TIME STANDS STILL

"It is a relief and a pleasure to see such thoughtful and well-crafted new writing on the stage. Mr. Margulies is a compassionate observer of human behavior. He reveals depths of tension through the most superficial tics. Beautifully written."

—STEVEN LEIGH MORRIS, *LA WEEKLY*

"Donald Margulies has crafted another beautifully bleak portrait of a tortured artist."

—MELISSA ROSE BERNARDO, *ENTERTAINMENT WEEKLY*

"In the plays of Donald Margulies, art and life often bump together fractiously. He's most interested in the friction that results when artistic imperatives vie with friends, lovers and the seductive pull of normalcy. And *Time Stands Still* is a Margulies story. It is an intelligent, perceptive, often funny, sometimes surprising, and always compelling piece of writing."

—PAUL HODGINS, *ORANGE COUNTY REGISTER*

"Donald Margulies's new play is a thoughtful, absorbing work."

—DAVID ROONEY, *VARIETY*

"If playwright Donald Margulies was competing with himself, his brilliant new play would win. Margulies conveys contemporary attitudes toward war, the media, and relationships by his skillful choice of characters who express themselves with bite and wit."

—LAURA HITCHCOCK, CURTAINUP

"Everything starts with Donald Margulies's smart, grown-up script, which blossoms onstage . . . A play that's a major and memorable dramatic experience."

—ROBERT FELDBERG, *RECORD* (NEW JERSEY)

"There's a mournful tug beneath the surface of *Time Stands Still*, but the material is also colloquial, lively and inquisitive without being preachy. This is a work that asks lots of questions—chiefly, about how much guilt and responsibility over wartime tragedies individuals can carry without going mad—while maintaining enough humility to know that it can't answer them. Instead of pontificating, the characters bicker, accuse and snipe, but they also defend one another, often tenderly. They also come off as believable relics of old-school, hard-core journalism, principled individuals who have perhaps poured too much of their hearts into what they do."

—STEPHANIE ZACHAREK, *NEW YORK* MAGAZINE

TIME STANDS STILL

BOOKS BY DONALD MARGULIES
AVAILABLE FROM TCG

Brooklyn Boy

Collected Stories

Dinner with Friends

God of Vengeance

Luna Park: Short Plays and Monologues
INCLUDES:
July 7, 1994
Luna Park
Nocturne
Pitching to the Star

Shipwrecked! An Entertainment—
The Amazing Adventures of Louis de Rougemont
(As Told by Himself)

Sight Unseen and Other Plays
INCLUDES:
Found a Peanut
The Loman Family Picnic
The Model Apartment
Sight Unseen
What's Wrong with This Picture?

TIME STANDS STILL | a play

Donald Margulies

THEATRE COMMUNICATIONS GROUP
NEW YORK
2010

This publication is made possible in part with public funds from the New York State Council on the Arts, a State Agency.

TCG books are exclusively distributed to the book trade by Consortium Book Sales and Distribution.

LIBRARY OF CONGRESS CATALOGING-IN-PUBLICATION DATA
Margulies, Donald.
Time stands still : a play / Donald Margulies.—1st ed.
p. cm.
ISBN 978-1-55936-365-5
eISBN 978-1-55936-668-7
1. Photojournalists—Drama. I. Title.
PS3563.A653T56   2010
812'.54—dc22   2010002007

Cover design by Lisa Govan
Cover photograph by Lynsey Addario
Text design and composition by Lisa Govan

First Edition, March 2010
4th printing

TIME STANDS STILL

PRODUCTION HISTORY

Time Stands Still was commissioned and given its world premiere by the Geffen Playhouse (Gilbert Cates, Producing Director; Randall Arney, Artistic Director; Susan Barton, Acting Managing Director) in Los Angeles, CA, on February 11, 2009. The director was Daniel Sullivan; the set design was by John Lee Beatty, costumes were by Rita Ryack, lighting was by Peter Kaczorowski, original music was by Peter Golub and the sound design was by Jon Gottlieb; the production stage manager was James T. McDermott and the stage manager was Jill Gold. The cast was as follows:

SARAH GOODWIN	Anna Gunn
JAMES DODD	David Harbour
RICHARD EHRLICH	Robin Thomas
MANDY BLOOM	Alicia Silverstone

Time Stands Still was produced on Broadway by Manhattan Theatre Club (Lynne Meadow, Artistic Director; Barry Grove, Executive Producer), in association with the Geffen Playhouse, by special arrangement with Nelle Nugent/Wendy Federman, at the Samuel J. Friedman Theatre on January 28, 2010. The direction and design team were the same as in Los Angeles, with the exception of the sound design, which was by Darron L. West; the production stage manager was Robert Bennett and the stage manager was Shanna Spinello. The cast was as follows:

SARAH GOODWIN	Laura Linney
JAMES DODD	Brian d'Arcy James
RICHARD EHRLICH	Eric Bogosian
MANDY BLOOM	Alicia Silverstone

ACKNOWLEDGMENTS

In addition to the aforementioned talented people who contributed immeasurably to the care and feeding of *Time Stands Still*, I would like to thank Lynsey Addario, Ethan Bronner, Brooke Gladstone, Lori Grinker, Fred Kaplan, Jack Saul, Bruce Shapiro, Lynn Street and Bob Woodruff, all of whom had insightful and inspiring things to say.

A special nod of thanks to Elisabet Klason, Björn Lönner, Malin Buska and Michel Riddez, the cast of the Playhouse Teater production in Stockholm, Sweden, where the play had its European premiere on October 2, 2009; the director was Anders Björne.

SARAH GOODWIN	a photojournalist, late thirties to early forties
JAMES DODD	a freelance journalist, late thirties to early forties
RICHARD EHRLICH	a photo editor, fifty-five
MANDY BLOOM	an event planner, twenty-five

THE SETTING

A loft in Williamsburg, Brooklyn. The present.

The space is raw, unfinished, resourcefully furnished, with nothing slick about it. Its decor reveals a good eye, wide travels, and limited budget. The space is open: cooking, dining, living, sleeping, working; a bathroom and the front door. At the start of the play, the housekeeping is wanting; someone left in a hurry.

When the play begins, Sarah is on crutches. One leg is in a soft cast, an arm is in a sling, and one side of her face is pocked with shrapnel. The action of the play spans about a year during which Sarah gradually recovers from her injuries.

To make for a more fluid reading experience, I have omitted notations that would instruct the actors when to overlap dialogue. In performance, the intended spoken effect is that of conversation by characters who know each other so intimately, they can anticipate and conclude each other's sentences.

Act One

1.

A loft in the Williamsburg section of Brooklyn. Winter. Night. The front door is unlocked and opened, casting light from the hallway. James, hauling duffles, and camera bags, helps Sarah, on crutches, inside. Both are winded, having climbed the stairs.

JAMES: Almost there . . . Atta girl . . . Watch the step.

SARAH: I see.

JAMES: How you doing? *(She nods)* You're doing great.

SARAH *(Sarcastic)*: Oh, yeah.

JAMES: There you go . . . *(He helps her into a chair)* And . . . she's *down*. The Eagle has landed. *(Exhausted, she nods and manages a smile)* *That* wasn't too bad, now was it?

SARAH: Piece a cake.

JAMES: Let's do this again sometime.

SARAH: Let's.

JAMES: Try it with an elevator next time.

(She smiles. A beat.)

SARAH *(Momentary alarm)*: Where are my cameras?

JAMES *(Reassuring)*: They're right here.

(A beat.)

You okay?

SARAH: Thirsty.

JAMES: Water, or uh . . . ?

SARAH: Water would be great.

JAMES: One water, coming up.

(He fills a glass. She removes her stocking hat. We see more clearly the scars on her face. He hands her the glass.)

SARAH: Thanks.

(He waits for her to drink it all down.)

JAMES: Okay?

(She nods while drinking.)

More?

(She shakes her head.)

SARAH: Thank you.

(She gives him her glass.)

JAMES: Hungry?

SARAH: Do we have anything?

(He looks in the refrigerator.)

JAMES: Uh . . . No. Nothing edible, anyway.

(He sniffs a container of spoiled milk, reacts to the stench.)

Uch.

SARAH: What.

(He pours the clotted milk down the drain.)

JAMES: I ran out of here so fast . . . I didn't have time to empty
the fridge . . . *(A take-out container)* Mmm! Want some
six-week-old calamari? I *think* it's calamari, could be
linguine.

SARAH: Don't worry about that now.

JAMES *(Shows her)*: Look. Gonna need dental records to iden-
tify *this* one.

SARAH: Jamie, really, just leave it.

(He abandons the task.)

JAMES: I'll go food shopping in the morning.

SARAH: That's fine.

JAMES: Unless you want me to run down now.

SARAH: No. Just . . . *(Gestures for him to relax)*

JAMES *(An idea)*: Hey how about a nightcap?

SARAH: I'd *love* a nightcap.

JAMES: Should be some scotch . . . *(He finds a bottle)* Yes.

(He pours two glasses. Silence.)

SARAH: Strange.

JAMES: What.

SARAH: Being here.

JAMES: I bet.

(His cell phone rings.)

SARAH: I don't want to talk to anybody.

JAMES *(Looks at his phone)*: It's Richard.

SARAH: Not even Richard.

JAMES: Oh, shit, he wanted me to call when we landed.

9

SARAH: You've had your hands full. He'll understand; call him in the morning.

(*James nods, turns off the phone, hands her the drink.*)

JAMES: Cheers, baby.
SARAH: Cheers.

(*They drink. Silence. She thinks of something that makes her laugh.*)

JAMES: What.
SARAH: The cab driver. Just now. What a character! Wasn't he?
JAMES: Uh-huh.
SARAH: What is it he said that cracked us up?
JAMES (*Recalling*): Oh, yeah, uh . . .
SARAH (*Remembering*): "Bottle cap."
JAMES: Right.
SARAH: He meant "bottleneck." "Bottle cap up ahead." I didn't know what the hell he was talking about.
JAMES: Me, neither.

(*Pause.*)

SARAH: Reminded me of Tariq.
JAMES: Oh, yeah?
SARAH: Didn't he remind *you* . . . ?
JAMES: No. Can't say he did.

(*A beat.*)

SARAH: Huh.

(*Pause. She touches his arm. He looks at her.*)

Thank you.

JAMES: For what?

SARAH: For everything. For getting me home, for being there.

JAMES: I *wasn't* there.

SARAH: For being there when I woke up. Thank you for that.

JAMES *(A rueful smile)*: Yeah, well, uh . . .

(He unpacks sundries and medications. Silence.)

SARAH: What happens tomorrow?

JAMES: Tomorrow? We sleep in. However long we like.

SARAH: What else?

JAMES *(Shrugs)*: Errands 'n' shit.

(Pause.)

SARAH: What happens day after that?

JAMES: Day after that's Doctors' Day. *My* shrink at nine, your
orthopedist at one . . .

SARAH: Goody . . .

JAMES: Neuro-guy at three-something . . . Physical Therapy
at five . . .

SARAH: I'm a real fun date, aren't I.

JAMES: Baby, you're the best.

(Pause.)

SARAH: And what happens after that?

JAMES: After that?

(She nods. Pause.)

We put you back together again.

(A beat. He kisses her forehead.)

Welcome home.

2. ____

A few days later. Late afternoon. James sits at the table typing on his laptop. Sarah, her laptop nearby, exercises her leg by raising and lowering it. We hear the sound of an arriving email.

JAMES: I just sent you something.

(*Sarah checks her email. She laughs.*)

SARAH: That's good.

(*Silence. The sound of a second email.*)

JAMES: I just sent you another one.
SARAH: I thought you were working.
JAMES: I am.

(*She reads the second email.*)

SARAH (*A tepid response*): Very funny.

(*A beat.*)

(*Regarding his work*) This that freelance piece?

JAMES: Uh-huh.

SARAH: What are you calling it?

JAMES: Oh, I don't know, "The New Cinema of Cruelty"? Something like that. They'll probably come up with a lame title of their own.

SARAH: "Cinema of . . . Cruelty"?

JAMES: "Cruelty," yeah. How horror movies are a good barometer for the political climate of their day? *You* know, like *Invasion of the Body Snatchers*: made in the fifties, remade in the seventies, and then that stinker from a few years back? They're all about xenophobia. And this *new* brand of horror is all about torture. And the one thing they all have in common, is people being punished for having sex.

SARAH: That's like every horror movie ever made.

JAMES: Exactly. Like Janet Leigh in *Psycho*: She sleeps with her lover on her lunch hour so you know she must die.

SARAH: I'll never forget that black bra.

JAMES *(À la Groucho)*: *You'll* never forget that black bra? *(A beat)* Anyway, nowadays, sexually active people in movies don't get off that easy. Now the promise of sex lures them into, not just perilous situations, but out-and-out torture chambers.

SARAH: So, what're you trying to say with this?

JAMES: Well, that . . . this trend . . . Teenagers *love* this stuff, you know; they see them two, three times. It's cathartic.

SARAH: "Cathartic"? or are they just *feeding* on images of horror?

JAMES: No, I think it helps them, I do. Look at the world these kids are growing up in! Terror, torture—this constant bombardment of graphic sadism. It's desensitizing after a while; loses its shock value.

SARAH: So, wait, you're saying it's desensitizing *and* cathartic?

JAMES: Yeah . . . I guess . . .

SARAH: Is that even possible? I mean, *can* something be desensitizing and cathartic at the same time? In order to experience catharsis, they have to be able to *feel* something, right?

JAMES: Yeah . . .

SARAH: But if they're desensitized . . . They're numb. Right? Isn't that what you're saying?

(A beat.)

JAMES: Uh-huh . . .

SARAH: So how . . . ? I don't know, sweetie . . . This seems a little . . . It's good; I think it's really good. But you might want to flesh it out a little bit more, don't you think?

(He thinks she's right—dammit. A beat.)

What time did you say he was coming?

(She begins the arduous process of getting up to go to the bathroom.)

JAMES: He *said* four.

SARAH: I need time to clean myself up.

JAMES: You know Richard: he's never on time.

SARAH: I wish you could have put him off.

JAMES: I did; for days. He's dying to see you.

SARAH: The last thing I want to do is chat.

(He comes to her aid.)

(Rejecting his help; sharp) Stop. *(Realizing she was harsh)* Jamie. Honey. Please. You're going to have to let me do things myself.

JAMES *(Backing off; softly)*: Okay.

(He tries to hide his attention to her journey to the bathroom.)

SARAH *(Her back to him)*: Stop. Staring. It only makes it worse.

JAMES *(Softly)*: Sorry I'm sorry.

(The downstairs buzzer sounds. He checks his watch.)

That's him.

SARAH: Fuck.

JAMES: Relax. It's only Richard. *(He buzzes back, unlocks the front door, and calls downstairs)* Come on up!

(She enters the bathroom and sees herself in the mirror.)

SARAH: I gotta do something about this face.

JAMES: Okay, hurry, he's on his way up.

*(She closes the door behind her.
James prepares coffee.
Richard enters.)*

RICHARD *(Warmly)*: Heyyyy!

JAMES: Hey.

(Richard gives him a bear hug.)

RICHARD: Boy am I glad to see *you!*

JAMES: Me, too.

RICHARD: Thank God you're home.

JAMES: I know!

RICHARD: Some nightmare, huh?

JAMES: Oh yeah.

RICHARD: Unbelievable. *(Lowers his voice)* Is she uh . . . ?
(Meaning: "Is she napping?")

JAMES: Bathroom.

RICHARD *(Looks toward the front door)*: C'mere, sweetie, it's okay . . .

(Two mylar balloons precede Mandy through the door-way.)

JAMES *(Surprised)*: Whoa!
MANDY *(Shyly)*: Hello.
RICHARD: Jamie, this is Mandy.
JAMES: Mandy. Hi.

(She starts to hug him.)

MANDY: Jamie.
JAMES *(Offering his hand)*: James.
MANDY: So nice to meet you finally!
JAMES: Nice to meet you, too.
MANDY: Richard talks about you guys all the time.
RICHARD *(Prompting James)*: I told you about Mandy. Re-
member I wrote you?
JAMES: Oh, yeah . . .
MANDY *(Regarding the balloons)*: These are for you, by the way.
JAMES: Oh, thanks.
MANDY: I didn't know which one to get: Welcome Back or
Get Well Soon, so I got both.
JAMES: They're great. Thank you. You want to give me your
uh . . . ? *(Meaning: "their coats")*

(He hangs up their coats.)

MANDY: I love your neighborhood!
JAMES: Oh, yeah? We were here way before it was cool.
RICHARD: Listen, thanks for having us.
JAMES: Of course.
MANDY *(Seconding Richard)*: Oh, yeah!
RICHARD: We're not going to stay long. I promise.
MANDY: We know you guys just got back and everything.
RICHARD: You just got back, I know you must be wrecked.

JAMES: No no, we're glad to see you; we'll see how long she holds up. Started physical therapy the other day . . .

RICHARD (*Understanding*): Oh . . .

JAMES: Really knocks the wind out of her.

RICHARD: Kick us out whenever you want. I just had to see her with my own eyes. Y'know?

JAMES (*Nods; then*): Try not to look shocked when you see her.

RICHARD (*Dreadfully*): Oh, no, really?

(*Mandy takes Richard's hand. A crutch falls in the bathroom.*)

JAMES (*Calls*): Honey?

SARAH (*Irritated, from off*): What?

JAMES: You okay in there?

SARAH (*Off*): Yes!

RICHARD: She certainly *sounds* like herself.

(*They laugh. A beat.*)

How was your flight?

JAMES: Turbulence you would not believe.

(*Richard groans.*)

MANDY: I hate that!

JAMES: Why those humongous airbuses don't routinely fall out of the sky, I do not know.

RICHARD: I know! I don't either!

JAMES (*To Mandy*): You know what I do when I hit turbulence like that—the really scary, rollercoaster kind? (*Mandy shakes her head*) I keep my eye on the flight attendant. I figure, as long as *she* looks cool . . .

MANDY: How'd this one look?

(*James bugs out his eyes in an impression of panic.*)

(*Laughing*) Oh, no!

RICHARD: How did Sarah do?

JAMES: Slept through most of the rough stuff, amazingly—
with the help of Percocet and one or two chasers, come
to think of it. Getting her from the hospital onto the
plane, though . . . *That* was . . .

RICHARD: Physically moving her you mean?

JAMES: Refusing a wheelchair, making a scene at the airport,
little things like that.

RICHARD: Oh, God. I can just see it.

JAMES: Plus the bureaucracy! Man! Between German effi-
ciency and American incompetence . . . ! You'd think
they never had to fly a wounded civilian home before.

RICHARD: The State Department was no help?

JAMES: Are you kidding? It was Kafkaesque. The maze of
bullshit they put me through! It was like *Brazil*.

RICHARD: "Central Services."

(Richard and James laugh.)

JAMES: "Central Services"! Right! *(To Mandy)* Have you ever
seen it?

MANDY: I've never been to South America.

JAMES: No, I mean . . .

RICHARD *(Gently)*: He means the *movie Brazil*.

MANDY: Oh. There was a movie?

JAMES: Terry Gilliam. Nineteen, what? Eighty . . . five?

RICHARD: Sounds right.

MANDY: *Brazil?*

JAMES: Futuristic Orwellian comedy-nightmare. Really worth
renting.

(Mandy jots it down in a small notebook.)

RICHARD: I wish you had let us help. The magazine could've
pulled a few strings.

JAMES: I know. I needed to bring her home myself. Y'know?

RICHARD *(Nods; then, discreetly, meaningfully)*: How are *you* doing?

JAMES *(Equivocally)*: Okay.

RICHARD: You are? Really? Are you sleeping?

JAMES: Pretty much.

RICHARD: No more of those dreams?

JAMES: Better.

RICHARD: So the meds are . . . ?

JAMES: Uh-huh.

RICHARD: Are you writing?

JAMES: Yeah . . . Sort of . . . Trying to . . .

RICHARD: What happened to that piece you were writing on spec?

JAMES: You mean the uh . . . ?

MANDY *(To Richard)*: What.

RICHARD: This terrific piece Jamie was writing.

MANDY: What about?

JAMES: The refugee situation in Syria and Jordan? What a catastrophe it is?

MANDY: Oh, wow.

JAMES: Gave me something to do while Sarah was in the hospital—or else I would've gone nuts.

RICHARD: I brought it up at a staff meeting, incidentally.

JAMES: You did?

RICHARD: There was a lot of interest.

JAMES: Really?

RICHARD: As soon as you can let me see it . . .

JAMES: Thanks, I will. I appreciate that.

(Sarah emerges from the bathroom wearing lipstick.)

SARAH: Hello-o-o.

(Richard, avoiding eye contact, goes to her. Mandy stands back, smiling shyly.)

RICHARD *(Brightly)*: Sarah!

SARAH *(Warmly)*: Richard!

JAMES: *There* she is!

RICHARD: *God*, it's good to see you.

SARAH: You, too.

RICHARD: Thought we lost you, kiddo. *(Embraces her too tightly)*

SARAH *(A gentle reminder)*: Careful.

RICHARD: Ooo. Sorry.

(Mandy gasps empathically. Sarah sees her for the first time.)

SARAH: Who's *this*?

JAMES: Mandy.

MANDY: I'm Mandy.

(Sarah looks quizzically at James.)

JAMES: Richard's new "friend."

RICHARD: Oh, I'm sorry. Sarah, this is my friend, Mandy.

MANDY: Hi.

SARAH: Hello.

MANDY: Such an honor to meet you!

SARAH: Thank you.

MANDY: Your pictures are awesome.

SARAH: *Thank* you.

MANDY *(Regarding the balloons)*: I brought these for you and Jamie.

SARAH *(Flatly)*: Oh isn't that nice.

JAMES *(Correcting Mandy)*: James.

MANDY: What?

JAMES: It's *James*.

MANDY: James! Right!

JAMES: You called me . . .

MANDY: Did I call you Jamie? *(James nods)* I keep doing that, don't I?

RICHARD: My fault. She hears *me* call you Jamie, so . . .

MANDY: *Richard* calls you Jamie, so I think of you as Jamie.

RICHARD: I forget, to the rest of the world you're James.

JAMES: That's all right, it's just this thing of mine.

MANDY: I understand. No, I do, completely.

> *(Regarding balloons; to Sarah) Anyway* . . . I know they're kinda silly.

SARAH: No no.

MANDY: But they have this amazing way of cheering people up.

SARAH *(Smiles. A beat)*: I feel better already. *(Sotto voce)* Jamie, would you uh . . .

JAMES: Certainly. *(He sets them aside)*

MANDY: I thought about bringing flowers, but flowers are such a pain 'cause then the person you're giving them to has to run to get a vase of water to put them in? And another nice thing about balloons, is you never have to worry about them dying.

RICHARD: Man—?

MANDY: Although the air *does* leak out after a while and they get all shriveled up and weird.

JAMES *(Moving right along)*: Coffee, anyone?

SARAH: Yes, please.

RICHARD: Not on my account.

JAMES: Already making it.

RICHARD: Okay, then, thanks.

JAMES: Don't thank me till you've tried it. *(To Mandy)* My coffee's lousy.

SARAH: He's not kidding.

RICHARD: Oh, I know.

SARAH: I still want some.

JAMES *(To Mandy)*: You want some? No guarantee it's drink-able.

MANDY: Not for me, thanks. *(Looking at Richard)* I'm trying to cut out caffeine.

JAMES *(To Mandy)*: Single malt?

MANDY: No no.

JAMES: Water?

SARAH *(To Richard)*: Hey.

MANDY: Water's great, thanks.

SARAH : Hey! Notice anything different?

RICHARD *(Uncertain)*: Um . . .

(She mimes holding a cigarette.)

SARAH: I'm not smoking!

RICHARD: Oh!

SARAH: When was the last time you saw me without a cigarette? I haven't had one in six weeks!

RICHARD: Good for you!

SARAH: I *was* unconscious for *two* of those weeks . . .

RICHARD: But still!

(James's passport on the table piques Mandy's curiosity.)

MANDY *(To James)*: You mind if I uh . . . ?

JAMES: Go right ahead.

MANDY: I love looking at people's passports; all the cool stamps and stuff? *(Regarding his photo)* Wow. I like you in a beard.

JAMES *(Flattered)*: Yeah? I've been thinking of growing it back.

SARAH: You have? *(He nods)* Since when? Two seconds ago?

JAMES: No, I uh . . .

MANDY *(Regarding the passport)*: God, *look* at this, you guys have been *every*where. Sudan . . . Sierra Leone . . . Congo!

RICHARD: She asked me; I couldn't re*mem*ber half the places you've been!

MANDY *(Showing James)*: What's this say?

JAMES: Kurdistan.

MANDY: Wow. When did you start doing this?

JAMES: Summer after college.

MANDY: Where'd you go to school?

JAMES: Stanford.

MANDY: Oh, wow.

JAMES: I was an economics major, with a minor in illegal sub-
stances. Looking at what: a year at Bear Stearns, then
on to business school? *(He shudders)* Two weeks after
graduation, I was on my way to Somalia.

MANDY: You joined the army?

JAMES: No, no, as a reporter. There I was: this stupid, cocky
kid with no idea what the fuck I was doing, filing stories from Mogadishu that started getting picked up,
and before I knew it, I was hooked. Cut to: one night,
like eight years ago, on my way home from the West
Bank, in the lobby of the American Colony Hotel in
East Jerusalem, there was this beautiful woman arguing with the desk clerk.

RICHARD *(Feigned ignorance)*: Gee, I wonder who that could
be?

JAMES: Needless to say, I did not go home.

(James kisses Sarah.)

MANDY: Aw . . . That is so cool.

(James sits with mugs of coffee for Richard and himself.)

JAMES: It's high-test; we're out of decaf.

RICHARD: That's fine.

(A beat.)

SARAH *(To James, regarding the coffee)*: Don't *I* get any?

JAMES: It's caffeinated.

SARAH: So?

JAMES: I'm afraid it'll keep you up.

SARAH: *So?*

JAMES: I thought you were worried about sleeping through
the night.

SARAH: No, *you* were worried about my sleeping through the night. I'm going to end up taking a Xanax anyway.

JAMES: How 'bout I make you a cup of green tea or something?

SARAH: I don't *want* a cup of green tea! All I want is a fucking cup of coffee!

(A beat. James gives her his.)

Thank you! Jesus . . .

(Awkward silence.)

RICHARD: You know, we really don't have to uh . . . ?

MANDY *(Picking up his cue to go)*: Oh. Totally.

SARAH: Mandy? What kind of work do you do?

MANDY: Me? Oh, it's really boring.

RICHARD: Public relations.

MANDY: What?! I do not!

RICHARD: No? Doesn't it fall under the heading of public relations?

MANDY: No it does not! *(To Sarah, regarding men)* Don't you love how they listen? I am not in PR. *(To Richard)* How could you even *think* that?

RICHARD *(Sheepish)*: I'm sorry, I thought . . .

MANDY *(To Sarah)*: I'm an event planner.

SARAH: A what?

MANDY: An event planner. Event planning is a field unto itself. You know: like arts events, book launches and stuff?

SARAH: Uh-huh.

MANDY: That's how I met Richard.

RICHARD: The Darfur book. Party was at MoMA.

MANDY: In the sculpture garden.

RICHARD: Gorgeous night.

MANDY: Very dramatic. Everything all lit up?

JAMES: Uh-huh.

MANDY: Sometimes we work pro bono for charities? *(Parenthetically)* That means we do it for nothing. Like, we did this masked ball for AIDS in Africa at the zoo?

SARAH: So you . . . ?

MANDY: I get to choose the location . . .

SARAH: Uh-huh . . .

MANDY: *You* know, like where? Come up with the theme . . .

RICHARD: She conceptualizes the whole thing!

MANDY: Work with the caterer, florists . . . help plan the menu . . .

RICHARD: I never thought twice about what goes *into* these things!

MANDY: Like, sometimes . . .

RICHARD: It's incredibly complicated!

MANDY *(Over Richard)*: Sometimes you want it to be some place you never in a million years would think of?

JAMES: Uh-huh.

MANDY: Like, one of my favorite spaces is the Egyptian rooms at the Met.

SARAH: Uh-huh?

MANDY: *You* know: with all the uh *(To Richard)* What's the word again, for all the mummies and stuff? Sar . . . ?

RICHARD, JAMES AND SARAH: Sarcophagi.

MANDY: Sarcophagi! Right! We had an after-party there. For a movie set in Egypt? It's like you're really there, in this spooky ancient place. King Tut's tomb or something. Really intense.

SARAH: I bet.

(A beat.)

I guess you can say *I'm* into events, too.

MANDY: You are?

SARAH: Wars, famines, genocides . . .

(*Mandy smiles but feels the sting.*
    James gives Sarah a look: "Good work.")

RICHARD (*Breaking the tension*): Oh, I almost forgot . . . *Every-*
    one at the magazine sends their love. They wanted me
    to give you this. (*He hands Sarah a greeting card*)
SARAH: Oh!

(*Richard takes the card out of its envelope for her to read.*)

RICHARD: They passed it around for everybody to sign.
SARAH: Sweet.
RICHARD: *You* know how it is: something bad happens, peo-
    ple feel helpless; they want to *do* something.
SARAH: I know. Thank them for me.
RICHARD: I will.
MANDY: I prayed for you.
SARAH: Hm?
MANDY: Even though we'd never met? I prayed for you.

(*A beat.*)

SARAH: Huh! (*Meaning: "How do you like that!"*)
MANDY: It's weird 'cause it's not like I believe in God or any-
    thing. 'Cause I don't. Not really. I don't think. But
    whenever I wish for something? Or want something
    really really bad? I talk to Him. Like when I was little
    and my grandpa got sick? I'd go to bed and lay there in
    the dark and say over and over, "Please God . . . please
    please please let Grandpa get better." When we heard
    about *you*—Richard was so upset—
SARAH: Were you, Richard?
RICHARD: Uy. (*Meaning: "You have no idea how upset."*)
MANDY: In all the time we'd been together, I'd never *seen* him
    so upset.
SARAH: How long is that?
MANDY (*To Richard, corroborating*): Three months?

RICHARD: Almost four.

MANDY *(Continuing)*: Anyway, he was so scared you'd be maimed or brain-damaged or something.

RICHARD: Hon . . . ?

MANDY: I found myself going, "Please God, Richard loves Sarah so much, *please* don't let her die."

(Richard squeezes Mandy's hand but she misreads his signal. Without missing a beat:)

Honey, you're hurting my hand.

RICHARD *(Changing topic; to Sarah)*: You look great, by the way.

SARAH: Yeah?

JAMES: Doesn't she?

SARAH: You like my *Phantom of the Opera* look?

RICHARD: No, you look wonderful.

MANDY: You really do!

SARAH *(To Richard)*: Is that why you haven't really looked at me since you got here?

RICHARD: What? I've been looking at you . . .

SARAH: Bullshit. Even now, you're looking somewhere north of my ear.

JAMES: Sarah . . . Really . . .

RICHARD *(Embarrassed)*: No I'm not.

MANDY: To tell you the truth? I expected much much worse.

SARAH: Gee. Thanks.

MANDY: I mean, you hear "scars" . . .

RICHARD *(Gently)*: Honey . . .

MANDY: You could always have, like, laser surgery or something. I mean, if they bother you.

SARAH *(Pointedly)*: They don't.

(A beat.)

MANDY: Oh. Okay. You mind if I uh . . . ? *(Referring to the bathroom)*

SARAH: Please.

MANDY *(Softly, to Richard)*: Be right back.

(Sarah and James watch Mandy and Richard kiss. Mandy goes to the bathroom. The remaining three sip coffee in silence.)

RICHARD *(Jocularly)*: Fuck you.

JAMES *(Feigned innocence)*: What!

SARAH *(Laughing)*: We didn't say anything!

RICHARD: You don't *have* to say anything. You guys are the worst poker faces ever.

SARAH: She's darling, Richard, really.

RICHARD: Don't give me that, you don't think she's "darling."

SARAH *(To James)*: Don't you think so? Don't you think she's darling?

JAMES: Adorable.

RICHARD: I knew you'd give me shit for this . . .

JAMES: She is!

SARAH: I think it's sweet: You always wanted a little girl.

(James is enjoying this.)

RICHARD *(To Sarah)*: I don't *care* you're on crutches, I will hurt you so bad . . . !

SARAH: Imagine my surprise: I wake up from *a coma* and Astrid is gone! Replaced by this . . . changeling! This sprite!

JAMES *(Remembering)*: Yeah! Good old Astrid!

RICHARD: Oh, *now* she's "good old . . ."

JAMES: I *liked* her.

SARAH: So did I.

RICHARD: You *hated* Astrid!

SARAH: I did not!

JAMES: Shhh . . . She can hear you in there.

SARAH *(Lower)*: I never said I *hated* her . . .

RICHARD: You called her the "attack-girlfriend"! Remember?

SARAH: Oh, yeah.

JAMES *(To Sarah)*: We did, didn't we.

(Sarah and James share a laugh.)

RICHARD: You accused me of *siccing* her on you; said I used her to act out my hostility.

JAMES: It's all coming back to me now.

RICHARD: Astrid was brilliant. Okay? But you know what? *Fuck* brilliant. I've *done* brilliant. I'm sick of analyzing every goddamn thing to death. Deciding where to go out to eat was like . . . arbitration. Maybe I got off on it once, arguing about *every*thing. Not anymore. Too much work. I want something *simple* for a change.

SARAH: Well, congratulations.

RICHARD: When have you *ever* approved of any relationship I've ever had? Huh? Never!

SARAH: This is not a "relationship," Richard, who are you kidding? You're *screw*ing this *girl*!

JAMES: Shhh . . . !

RICHARD *(Lower)*: What kind of man do you think I am? One of those creepy middle-aged guys who prey on women half their age? I *hate* guys like that! Just because she's young.

SARAH: I have no problem with her being young.

RICHARD: You were young once, too, you know . . . You were her age when I hired you as my intern! Younger, even!

SARAH: Not like *that*! . . .

JAMES: Shhh! . . .

SARAH *(Lower)*: I was never like *that* . . . There's young and there's . . . embryonic. This girl is a lightweight. She's a lightweight, Richard.

RICHARD: Make fun all you want! There is nothing remotely cynical about her. She's guileless. Open.

JAMES: And very hot.

RICHARD: Yes! She's hot! Okay?

JAMES: Shhh!

RICHARD (*Lower*): Richard's got himself a hot girlfriend! How do you like that? Now I'll know what it's like! I can die happy. Look: I love you and I'm glad you're alive, but you know what? I don't give a shit what you think.

JAMES: Fair enough.

(Pause.)

RICHARD: She delights me.

SARAH: Good.

RICHARD: She's . . . fun! She's light. I discovered I *like* those things. I *missed* them. I'd lived without sunlight for so long during The Astrid Years . . . It was like going from black and white to color. Like being in East Berlin when the wall came down. I met Mandy and I said, "Yes!" And I never would have let myself go for it if it wasn't for you.

SARAH: Me?

RICHARD: Almost dying like that. Shook me to the core. Nothing puts things in perspective like a near-death experience.

SARAH: Yeah. Preferably someone else's.

(Mandy emerges from the bathroom.)

MANDY: I love the soap you have in there! *(Holds her hand to Richard's nose)* Smell this. *(He does)* Isn't that cool?

RICHARD: Mm. *(He kisses her hand.)*

MANDY *(To Sarah)*: Where did you get it? Someplace exotic, I bet.

SARAH: Depends on how you feel about The Body Shop.

MANDY *(Embarrassed)*: Oh. I thought maybe you brought it back from the Middle East or something.

(Sarah shakes her head. A beat.)

RICHARD *(To Sarah)*: I was over at ICP the other day. *(Meaning: the International Center for Photography)*
SARAH: Oh, yeah?
RICHARD: Everybody's very excited you're home. They'd be thrilled to have you teach a class, you know.
SARAH: Oh, really?
RICHARD: I said I would talk to you. Whenever you're able. Ideally, they'd love to have you in residence for a year.
SARAH: A year? I couldn't give them a *year* . . .
RICHARD: Why not?
SARAH: I don't expect to *be* here in a year.
RICHARD: What do you mean? Where will you be?
SARAH: Where do you think?

(A beat.)

RICHARD: You're not serious.
SARAH: You know me pretty well . . . You don't expect me to sit around for a whole *year* . . . If I really work my ass off in rehab, I could be back by spring.
RICHARD *(To James)*: You're encouraging this?
JAMES: I'm going with her.
RICHARD: Are you out of your fucking minds? Both of you!
MANDY *(Calming)*: Sweetie . . .
RICHARD *(To Sarah)*: *You* almost died . . .
SARAH: Richard . . .
RICHARD *(To James)*: *You* had a fucking *break*down . . .
JAMES: Not a "breakdown" . . .
RICHARD *(To Mandy)*: They're the Sid and Nancy of journalism!
MANDY *(Aside, to Richard)*: Who are Sid and Nancy?
RICHARD *(Patiently)*: Sid Vicious. Punk rocker. And his girlfriend. Famous drug addicts, long dead. *(To James and Sarah)* What more has to happen? Huh, guys?

SARAH: Richard . . .

RICHARD: How many close calls before you say, "Fuck this, I'm staying home"?

SARAH: You don't get it, you never did.

RICHARD: Oh, please, haven't you done enough penance for your trust fund?

JAMES: All right . . . Okay . . .

RICHARD: So your daddy's rich. Get over it!

SARAH: What does my father's money have to do with it?

RICHARD: Don't give me some crap how this is a calling. It's no calling, it's more like a death wish.

SARAH: Why do I do what I do? Because I have so little regard for life? Does that make any sense?

RICHARD: I didn't say you had little regard for life, but you sure as hell don't have much regard for your own!

(Silence.)

MANDY: Ooo. You know what I would *love?*

(The others look at her. A beat.)

JAMES: What.

MANDY: Do you have any ice cream?

JAMES: Ooo, sorry, no we don't.

MANDY *(To Richard)*: I could really go for some *dulce de leche* . . .

RICHARD: You want ice cream, baby? I'll get you ice cream.

MANDY: I can go, just tell me where.

RICHARD: No, honey, you stay.

JAMES: No, no, I'll do it. There's a market right on the corner.

RICHARD: I'll go with you.

JAMES: You really don't have to; it'll take me a minute.

RICHARD: I'll keep you company.

(He gets his and James's coats.)

MANDY: Is this really a pain?

JAMES: Not at all. *(To Sarah)* You okay if I uh . . . ?

SARAH: Fine. Go. Hunt. Gather.

JAMES: We'll be right back.

(James and Richard go.)

MANDY *(Calls as they go downstairs)*: Bye! Thank you!

(Mandy and Sarah are left in awkward silence.)

You guys seem to have such a great marriage.

SARAH: Oh, we're not married.

MANDY: You're not? I thought . . .

SARAH: No, we've been together for eight and a half years but we never actually bothered to make it legal.

MANDY: Oh. Wow. I thought . . .

SARAH: No. Too busy saving the world.

MANDY: I don't know how you go to these places. *War* zones.

SARAH: Not as hard as you might think. War was my parents' house all over again; only on a different scale.

MANDY: It must be so intense. I mean, how you can even concentrate with all that going on?

SARAH: It's so automatic, I don't even think about it. When I look through that little rectangle . . . Time stops. It just . . . All the noise around me . . . Everything cuts out. And all I see . . . is the picture.

MANDY: Your pictures are beautiful.

SARAH: Thank you.

MANDY: I don't mean "beautiful," I mean . . . *You* know . . .

SARAH: You can call them beautiful . . . *I* think they're beautiful. But then I'm their mother.

(Pause.)

MANDY: Um. Listen, I know how much you and Richard mean to each other.

SARAH: Mandy, you really don't have to . . .

MANDY: I know; Richard told me.

(A beat.)

SARAH: That was twenty years ago.

MANDY: Yeah but you stayed *friends*. That's wonderful. And *I* come along and it's like: "Who is *she*? Oh, she must be Richard's mid-life crisis."

SARAH: No . . .

MANDY: Well, I'm not. Okay? Whatever it was that brought us together, we're together. For real. This is not a passing "thing." I *love* Richard. He is a very good man.

SARAH: Yes he is.

MANDY: Probably the nicest man I've ever known. He's smart, and kind, and caring. And I love his voice; I love the way he *sounds*. So he's a lot older than me. So what? It's not like I go around thinking, "Oh my God, he's like three years younger than my dad!" 'Cause I don't. All that matters—to *me*, anyway—is he takes care of me. He makes me feel safe. And one day, when he's old, and demented?, I'll take care of *him*. *(A beat)* Look. I know I have a lot to learn.

SARAH: Mandy . . .

MANDY: I *know* that. I'm *totally* provincial. My world is like *this* big. *(Makes a small globe with her hands)* And yours is like . . . *(She enlarges her imaginary globe)*

SARAH: Right now my world is as big as from here to the bathroom. I've got to get this leg working like a leg again.

(She stands and walks around.)

MANDY: You are so brave.

SARAH: Oh, please. Don't call me brave.

MANDY: You are. How many people could do what you do?

SARAH: I know what bravery looks like and, believe me, this is not bravery. This is dumb luck. An occupational hazard.

MANDY: What happened? I mean, Richard told me a little . . . You don't have to talk about it . . .

SARAH: Roadside bomb. I got thrown I don't know how many feet into the air. One of my cameras turned up like forty yards away.

MANDY: Oh, wow.

SARAH: Head full of shrapnel, banged up this leg pretty good. Medivac'ed to Germany. Kept in a coma till the swelling went down . . .

MANDY: It was great Jamie was there—I mean James.

SARAH: Jamie was *here*. He'd come home. Four or five weeks earlier. He flew over after.

MANDY: Oh. I thought he was with you.

SARAH *(Shakes her head, then)*: Something happened. He . . . needed to get home.

(Mandy nods. Pause.)

MANDY: Sorry about your friend.

SARAH *(Distracted)*: Hm?

MANDY: Didn't you have a friend? You were with?

SARAH: Yeah. My fixer.

MANDY: Your what?

SARAH: Fixer. That's what we call interpreters over there: fixers. Guides. Go-betweens. They make contacts, talk to the locals, set up interviews. They take care of everything for us. Everything. We're lost without them.

MANDY: He was right next to you? *(Sarah doesn't respond)* That must've been horrible.

SARAH: Actually, I don't remember. All I know is, there he was . . . next to me . . . *(Pause)* And I never saw him again.

MANDY: Wow.

(Long pause.)

SARAH: He was an engineering student—before it all went to hell. *(A beat)* Taught himself American English by reading *A Farewell to Arms* over and over again. Carried it with him wherever he went. That and the Koran. *(A beat)* He had a wife. Who was killed. And two little girls. Also killed. About a year into the war. A mortar attack on their apartment building while he was at school. *(A beat)* He was a lovely, lovely, man. Funny! And he *loved* America. Loved it. Everything about it. Television.

(Pause. Sarah's mind is elsewhere.)

MANDY: What was his name?

(Pause. Sarah looks at Mandy.)

SARAH: His name was Tariq.

(James and Richard are heard coming up the stairs. They enter, hang up their coats.)

RICHARD *(Off)*: That's amazing!
JAMES *(Entering)*: I know; it's a miracle.
RICHARD *(Entering; to Sarah)*: Your cameras made it?!
JAMES: I was just telling Richard . . .
SARAH: My Canon and my Leica. My panoramic was lost.
RICHARD: Still, that's incredible.
JAMES *(To Mandy)*: No *dulce de leche*; I got vanilla.
MANDY: That's okay. Thank you.

(James notices the lingering, sober look on Sarah's face.)

JAMES *(Sotto voce to Sarah)*: You okay?
SARAH: Yeah.

(James scoops ice cream into bowls.)

RICHARD: What about your pictures?

SARAH: I've got a bunch on my laptop, plus thousands more I have yet to download.

MANDY: Wow!

RICHARD: You want me to take care of it?

SARAH: No . . .

RICHARD: I'll have someone at the office do it.

SARAH: That's all right. Gives me something to do.

RICHARD *(Referring to her laptop)*: Can I see?

SARAH *(Shrugs)*: Go ahead.

JAMES: Now?

RICHARD: No?

SARAH: Why not?

JAMES: Why don't we wait till next time?

RICHARD: Oh. Okay.

SARAH *(To James)*: Why? What's the big deal?

JAMES *(To Richard)*: *Next* time. Okay? When Sarah's not . . .

SARAH: When Sarah's not what?

JAMES: I thought you were feeling jet-lagged.

SARAH: I'm wide awake. *(To Richard)* Here. *(Prepares her pictures for viewing on the laptop)*

JAMES: I really don't think this is a good idea.

SARAH: Richard's my editor; I want him to see my pictures.

JAMES: He came here to *see* you, now you're putting him to work?

SARAH: It was his idea!

RICHARD: Look, guys, I'm sorry I started this.

JAMES: Make a date for later this week, show him all the pictures you want.

SARAH: Why are you being such a dick?

JAMES: Honey? Really. Is this wise? It'll only upset you.

SARAH: *I'm* fine; *you're* the one who seems upset.

RICHARD: We don't have to do this now.

SARAH: No, we're doing it.

MANDY *(To Sarah)*: Can I see?

SARAH: Sure.

(Richard and Mandy view the slideshow in silence. We do not see the images. Richard's appreciation is more clinical: his profession is looking at pictures.)

MANDY *(To herself, regarding a photo)*: Mm. *(Pause. Another photo)* Huh. *(Pause. Another)* Oh, wow.

(Richard clicks to the next but Mandy stops him.)

Wait. Go back. *(A beat)* Okay.

(Richard clicks to the next.)

RICHARD: Oh, man, these are great, Sarah.
SARAH: Thanks.
JAMES: More coffee? *(No response)* Anyone?
RICHARD: What are you going to do with them?
SARAH: I don't know, I really haven't given it much . . .
RICHARD: You can't just sit on them, they're too good. *(An idea)* Why don't we do a book?
SARAH: A book?
RICHARD: A dual memoir. Your pictures, Jamie's commentary.
JAMES: My commentary? That means I would have to write it.
RICHARD: That's exactly what it means.
JAMES: What makes you think I want to revisit that stuff?
RICHARD: Maybe you should; maybe it would be good for you.
JAMES: What're you, my shrink?
SARAH *(To Richard)*: I don't know how you expect us to peddle around a book; I'm in no shape to do *that* . . .
RICHARD: You don't have to do a thing; I'll do all the footwork. Just give me your blessing to take it around. If our imprint passes—which I seriously doubt—Aperture would do it in a heartbeat.
SARAH: What makes you so sure?
RICHARD: First of all, the work is fantastic and, don't forget, darlin', for a couple of days there, you were national news.

SARAH: I know! I *had* my fifteen minutes, and spent it unconscious.

(They laugh.)

MANDY *(Shocked by a photo)*: Oh my God.

SARAH: Which one?

MANDY: The mother crying over her child? Are those burns?

SARAH: Yeah.

MANDY: Is he dead?

SARAH: Not yet. He was in shock. He died a few minutes later.

RICHARD: Great shot.

SARAH: Thanks.

MANDY *(Appalled; to Richard)*: How can you be so . . . ? *(Meaning: "matter-of-fact")*

RICHARD: What.

MANDY: That poor little boy! Maybe if she took him to the hospital instead of taking his picture . . .

RICHARD *(Gently)*: Honey . . .

SARAH: Rescue workers were there for that.

MANDY: But how could you just *stand* there?!

RICHARD: Shhh . . .

SARAH: I *wasn't* just standing there.

MANDY: The boy was dying! He was dying!

SARAH: The boy would have died no matter what I did. And I wouldn't have gotten the picture.

MANDY: You could have been helping them.

SARAH: I *was* helping them; I was taking their picture.

MANDY: How is that helping them?!

SARAH: By gathering evidence. To show the world. If it weren't for people like me . . . the ones with the cameras . . . Who would know? Who would care?

(Pause. Mandy gets a tissue from her handbag.)

MANDY: I saw this nature thing on TV about Africa? There was a sandstorm and this baby elephant got separated from his mother. It was so sad! She was there! You could see her! But there was like a dune and they couldn't find each other. The poor little guy was so lost and so scared . . . You *know* he'll never survive out there without his mother. But the movie people did nothing! They just kept filming!

SARAH: That's what they were there to do: the camera's there to *record* life. Not change it. Animals perish in the wild. That's life. And it's really sad, and unfair—but there's nothing we can do about it. The elephant was meant to die.

MANDY: How do *you* know? Are you God?

RICHARD: Honey . . .

MANDY: They could've saved him! A whole crew was *standing* there watching!

SARAH: The *camera* was there. You can't expect photographers to step into the frame and fix things they don't like. We're supposed to capture truth, not stage it.

MANDY: Couldn't they have made an exception, just this once?

RICHARD *(Tenderly)*: Oh, sweetie . . .

MANDY: They could've just brought him closer so she could *sniff* him! That's all it would take! She could have found him! They could have saved his life!

(Mandy breaks down in tears. Richard comforts her.)

RICHARD *(Soothing)*: Oh, baby . . .

(Pause.)

SARAH: I wish I could cry like that. But I can't; I can't let it get to me. If I let it get to me . . . How could I do my job? I couldn't. I'd want to take away the guns and rescue all the children. But I can't. That's not why I'm there.

(Pause.)

I'm there to take pictures.

3. ___

A few minutes later. Richard and Mandy are gone. James gathers bowls and mugs and rinses them at the sink. Mid-conversation:

SARAH: When did he tell you?

JAMES: When we went down for ice cream.

SARAH: He didn't want me to know?!

JAMES: He said I could tell you, he just didn't want to get into it while they were here.

SARAH: Why not?

JAMES: He was protecting Mandy.

SARAH: From what?

JAMES: From you.

SARAH: Was I really so horrible?

JAMES: You were pretty bad.

SARAH: We were buddies by the time they left . . .

JAMES: He was afraid of what you might say.

SARAH: What, that having a child at his age is the most ridiculous, irresponsible thing I've ever heard?

JAMES: *Something* like that, yeah.

SARAH: Did he talk about the morality of depriving a kid of a father?

JAMES: How is he depriving a kid of a father?

SARAH: He's too old! He'll be lucky if he lives to see the kid go off to college.

JAMES: What, young men don't die? Come on, Sarah, you know better than *that* . . .

SARAH *(Abashed)*: You're right.

JAMES: Anything could happen, to anyone, any time. You're living proof of that. A crane could come crashing down on us right now. If he's up for it, at this stage of his life, more power to him.

SARAH: So what are they going to do?

JAMES: He's going to marry her . . .

SARAH: Oh, my God.

JAMES: And they're going to have this baby.

SARAH: Poor Richard.

JAMES: Why "poor Richard"? The man is ecstatic; I've never *seen* him like this. He can't believe his good luck. To tell you the truth . . . When he told me . . . *(A beat)* I was jealous.

SARAH: Why, *you* wanted to get Mandy pregnant?

JAMES: Ha ha. No. *(A beat)* I wished *we* were getting married.

(Pause.)

SARAH: Seriously? *(He nods. A beat)* Oh, honey . . .

JAMES: Why not?

SARAH: I thought we didn't *need* marriage.

JAMES: We didn't.

SARAH: I thought we agreed.

JAMES: We did.

SARAH: It wasn't our thing.

JAMES: But things are different now.

SARAH: Why, because I almost died?

JAMES: Yes. *(Pause)* When you were in the hospital, I had no legal relationship to you whatsoever. Every catheter, every procedure, permission had to come from your asshole father. Do you realize how frustrating that was? I was right there! They had to get him on the phone from Palm Springs! *(A beat)* We've been putting ourselves in dangerous situations for years and never stopped to think what would happen if one of us got hurt. We didn't have a plan.

SARAH: So being married would've made medical management a lot easier.

JAMES: Yes.

SARAH: That's got to be the most romantic proposal I've ever heard.

(James laughs. Pause. He gets down on one knee.)

JAMES: Sarah . . .

SARAH *(Outraged)*: Get up. Get up! You're changing the rules on me!

JAMES: I'm not changing the rules, the playing field changed.

SARAH: You know how I feel about this! You can't lay this on me all at once! It isn't fair!

JAMES: I didn't mean to.

SARAH: What do you expect me to say, "Sure, honey, let's do it"?

JAMES: Of course not. *(A beat)* I had a lot of time to think while you were in the hospital, you know. I got to play out your death almost every single day. You were out for most of it, so you have no idea how close you came.

(A beat.)

When a couple gets to be our age, and has been together as long as we have, and witnessed what we have, and *survived* what we have, it's time to call this what it is: a marriage. *(A beat)* We are not your parents.

(Pause.)

SARAH: Can I think about it?

JAMES *(Deadpan)*: No. Of course you can think about it. *(He kisses her)* Take all the time you need.

(He resumes washing dishes. Long silence.)

SARAH: James? *(He can't hear her over the running water)* Jamie?

JAMES: Yeah?

SARAH: Come here a minute.

JAMES: One second . . . Let me just . . .

SARAH: *Now.* Please.

(He turns off the water, wipes his hands and joins her.)

JAMES: What is it?

SARAH: If we're going to do this . . . If we're really going to take this marriage talk seriously . . .

JAMES *(Bracing himself)*: Okay . . .

(Pause.)

SARAH: When I was there . . . After you left . . .

JAMES: I know what you're going to say.

SARAH: What do you mean you know?

JAMES: I *know.*

SARAH: You don't know what I'm going to say.

JAMES: He's dead. It happened. It's over.

(He kisses her brow and returns to the sink. Pause.)

SARAH *(Nonplussed)*: What the fuck just happened?

JAMES: I'm saying it's okay, I understand, I forgive you.

SARAH: You for*give* me? You for*give* me?

JAMES: Look . . . Whatever happened . . .

SARAH: I thought you knew what happened.

JAMES: Sarah. All I'm saying is . . . You're alive, you're here, we're together . . . That's all that matters.

(Pause.)

SARAH: Who told you? *(He makes a sound of exasperation)* People knew. Friends there knew.
JAMES: What difference does it make?
SARAH: I want to know who told you.
JAMES: No one had to tell me. I just knew.
SARAH: How?
JAMES: Please, Sarah, leave it alone? Please . . . ?
SARAH: Did I let something slip?
JAMES: Why are you pursuing this?
SARAH: I need to know.

(Pause.)

JAMES: Subtle things.
SARAH: Like . . . ?
JAMES: The tone of your voice on the phone.
SARAH: What.
JAMES: Changed.
SARAH: My tone.
JAMES: Yeah. Your voice kinda . . . Flattened out. Sounded farther away. Like you were holding something back.
SARAH: I was angry with you.
JAMES: I know you were angry.
SARAH: *That's* what you heard in my voice: I was mad at you.
JAMES: I know. But it wasn't just anger; I recognize your anger, believe me.
SARAH: That was it? My tone?

(Pause.)

JAMES: There was this email you sent.

SARAH: When?

JAMES: I don't know, like a week after I came home?

SARAH: Yeah . . . ?

JAMES: You wrote about all the checkpoints you hit, how insane it was. Something like that. Remember?

SARAH: Vaguely. So?

JAMES: The thing was . . . You wrote "I" instead of "we."

SARAH: What do you mean?

JAMES: In your emails. Whenever you described things you did, you always said "we." "*We* went here . . . *We* saw this . . ."

SARAH: I don't understand what that has to do with anything.

JAMES: One day it was "we," like it always was; the next day it was "I." *(Sarah looks quizzical)* "I." As if you were alone.

SARAH: I *was* alone. You were gone.

JAMES: No no. You *weren't* alone; Tariq was with you. You knew I knew he was with you; that was no secret.

SARAH: So?

JAMES: So something must have happened. Overnight. The status of your relationship changed. You weren't a photographer traveling with her fixer anymore. "We" took on a whole new meaning. Got way too intimate. You thought you could hide behind the first person singular. Instead you gave yourself away.

(Pause.)

SARAH: Wow. I'm impressed.

(Pause.)

JAMES: Look . . . These things happen.

SARAH: These things.

JAMES: We both know what it's like covering a war. It's pure adrenaline. Bombs bursting in air, death everywhere. We had some amazing sex, you and I.

SARAH: You think this is about sex?

JAMES: Well . . . ?

SARAH: I didn't just sleep with him.

JAMES: What do you mean?

SARAH: I didn't just *sleep* with him, James.

(He's perplexed. She averts her eyes. He understands.)

JAMES *(Stunned, hurt; to himself)*: Oh my God.

SARAH *(Reaches for him)*: Jamie . . .

JAMES: You were in *love* with him? *(Suddenly emotional)* How could you have fallen in love with him, Sarah? How could you have done that?!

SARAH: I don't know!

(Pause.)

JAMES: Why?

SARAH: When you left . . .

JAMES: Do you think I *wanted* to leave you? Do you?

SARAH: Of course not.

JAMES: I was a mess! Don't you remember what a mess I was?!

SARAH: Yes . . .

JAMES: I was shell-shocked!

SARAH: I know.

JAMES: That was real, that wasn't an act.

SARAH: I know it was real.

JAMES: Those women, those girls, blew up right there, right in front me!

SARAH: I know.

JAMES: Their blood and brains got in my eyes! In my mouth!

SARAH: I know.

JAMES: I freaked out! I had to get the hell out of there! Where were you for me?!

SARAH: I couldn't leave with you!

JAMES: Why, because of fucking Tariq?

SARAH: No! Because I had a job to do! You said you'd be okay without me!

JAMES: What was I *supposed* to say?!

SARAH: You told me to do what I had to do!

JAMES: What a joke! I leave you with our trusty fixer! "Tariq'll take care of you." Hell, that's what we *paid* him for! Two hundred bucks a day! Tell me something: Did you continue paying him? Even after you started fucking him?

(Long silence.)

Y'know . . . ? That terrible night, when I got the call . . . That you were hurt? . . . And he was dead? . . . You know the first thing that went through my head? *(She shakes her head)* I thought, "Oh, good! Now I can redeem myself for wimping out."

SARAH: You didn't wimp out.

JAMES: "I'll prove to Sarah how much she needs me. I'll *show* her!" Isn't that fucked?

SARAH: No . . .

JAMES: You'd just gotten blown up and I'm thinking, "Oh, good! A second chance!" *(A beat)* Never thought I'd be competing with a dead man.

(He grabs his jacket.)

SARAH: Where are you going?!

JAMES *(Softly)*: I gotta get out of here.

(He starts to go.)

SARAH *(Calls)*: James!

(She instinctively goes after him, and falls. James rushes to her aid.)

JAMES: Oh, shit . . .

SARAH: I fell.

JAMES: Yes. You did.

(He helps her up and carries her to the bed.)

SARAH: I'm okay, I'm okay. *(Pause)* You sure you want to marry me? Like *this*?

JAMES *(Smiling)*: Are you kidding? *Especially* like this. I can out run you for once. *(Pause. His smile fades)* I'm so sorry.

SARAH: Shhh . . .

JAMES: I should have stayed, I should never have gone home.

(She kisses his mouth to silence him. Their kissing becomes more intense. They whisper between kisses:)

I missed you.

SARAH: Missed you, too.

JAMES: I missed *this*.

SARAH: Me, too. *(Modestly)* Can we uh . . . ? *(Gestures to the lamp)* I don't want you to see me.

JAMES: I *want* to see you.

SARAH *(Insisting)*: Please.

(He turns off the light.)

JAMES: Are you okay with this?

SARAH: Yes.

JAMES: You sure? 'Cause if you're not ready . . .

SARAH: No no, I am. I want to.

(But she's not looking at him. In the semi-darkness, they begin to make love.
    The lights fade to black.)

Act Two

<u>1.</u>

Spring Evening. Four months later. The detritus of James and Sarah's wedding celebration: a partly eaten cake, discarded cups, plates, wine and champagne bottles, flowers, a CONGRAT-ULATIONS banner, etc. A flat-screen TV is a new addition to the room. Furniture has been rearranged to accommodate dozens of guests, the last of whom Sarah has escorted downstairs. Mandy, her pregnancy showing, tidies as best she can in her current state, throwing trash into a Hefty bag. With the others pitching in, the room is restored by the end of the scene. James and Richard have a buzz on. Mid story:

JAMES *(Wearily)*: This thing went on and on . . . And there were all these fucking monologues!

RICHARD: Uy. *(Meaning: "How tedious.")*

JAMES: Middle Eastern–looking man stands in a spotlight telling some horror story, *you* know, some *atrocity* that took place in his village . . .

RICHARD: Uh-huh.

JAMES: . . . or, uh, women in burkas talking about honor killings, how their fathers tried to hack them to death 'cause their brothers raped them . . .

MANDY *(Holding up an empty bottle)*: Excuse me? Recycling? *(James gets up)* Don't get up. Just tell me where.

(James shows her.)

RICHARD: Honey, come sit down.

MANDY: I can't when there's a mess.

JAMES *(Continuing, to Richard)*: The thing is, I *know* the people they put onstage . . . I *know* them, I've *lived* with them, *both* of us have. So seeing them turned into anthropologic curiosities, like dioramas in a museum, bathed in this romantic Caravaggio light with, *you* know: hallowed, Persian-sounding music . . .

(Sarah, in a smart dress [not a bridal gown], enters, walking with a cane.)

SARAH: What . . . ?

JAMES: The play the other night.

SARAH *(Unenthused)*: Uh.

RICHARD *(To Sarah)*: Did you hate it, too?

SARAH: Not as much as *he* did. *(To Mandy)* He *hates* plays. He's like one of those miserable men you see at matinees whose wives force them at gunpoint. *(Mandy laughs)*

JAMES: It's like you're trapped! Those fucking seats: you can never leave.

SARAH: I need a drink. Stat. *(She helps herself)*

JAMES *(To Sarah)*: They gone?

SARAH: Gone. In a town car, on their way to JFK.

JAMES: Thank God.

MANDY: Who?

JAMES: Her father.

SARAH: My father and his new wife. Evita.

MANDY: Is her name really Evita?

SARAH: Evelyn. My little joke.

MANDY: Oh. Duh.

JAMES *(To Sarah)*: You'd better watch it: You're going to call her Evita to her face one of these days.

SARAH: I think I already have.

RICHARD *(To James, resuming their discussion)*: Wait, I want to know why you went to this thing in the first place.

JAMES: Everybody was telling us we had to see it.

RICHARD: Busman's holiday, no?

SARAH: It got that incredible review.

RICHARD: I saw that.

JAMES: "Shattering!" "Unforgettable!"

SARAH: Place was packed!

JAMES: People are dying to be shattered. They'll pay a hundred *bucks* to be shattered.

MANDY: I like musicals. I don't know why people would pay all that money to be depressed.

JAMES: I'm with you, kid.

(Sarah picks up trash.)

MANDY *(To Sarah)*: Sit; it's *your* wedding . . .

SARAH: *You* sit; all that bending can't be good for you.

MANDY: I'm fine; I've been doing all this prenatal pilates.

JAMES *(Resuming, to Richard)*: Anyway, what I'm saying is . . .

RICHARD: What *are* you saying?

SARAH *(To Richard)*: How long has he been carrying on like this?

JAMES: It's not truth! *(Too loud)* It's kitsch!

SARAH: Shhh . . . Inside voice.

JAMES: Fake, sentimental shit that *passes* for truth! People *trick* themselves into thinking they're having an authentic experience when it's completely manufactured! Hell on earth made palatable—*packaged*—as an evening's entertainment!

RICHARD: But people are *seeing* it, though, right? I mean, isn't that encouraging? They want to be informed.

JAMES: *These* people don't need to be informed . . . *They* read
the paper, *they* listen to NPR . . . The ones who *should*
be seeing it, the *mujahideen* and the Taliban, let's face
it, don't get to the theater much. So it's that favorite
lefty pastime: preaching to the choir! They sit there,
weeping at the injustice, and stand at the end shouting:
"Bravo!" con*grat*ulating themselves for en*dur*ing such
a grueling experience, and go home feeling like they've
actually *done* something, when in fact *all* they've done
is assuaged their liberal guilt!

SARAH *(Sotto voce, to James)*: Are you finished?

RICHARD: What're you saying, these stories are off-limits to
anyone but people like you who have been on the front-
lines?

JAMES: No, of course not.

RICHARD: They shouldn't be told at all?

JAMES: I don't know, Richard, I don't have the answers.

RICHARD: Ah!

SARAH *(Changes subject)*: So, you want to hear what my father
just said to me downstairs? His parting words?

MANDY: What.

SARAH: He said there was something "unseemly" about a
couple who have been living in sin for nine years throwing themselves a wedding.

JAMES: Fuck him.

RICHARD: Is that what he said, "living in sin"?

SARAH: He said all it is is begging for gifts.

JAMES: We *said* no gifts!

SARAH: I know.

JAMES: If he felt compelled to give *any*thing, he should make
a donation to his favorite charity.

SARAH: Yeah, like the Christian Coalition.

JAMES *(To Richard)*: He is such an asshole.

SARAH: *Why* did I invite him?

JAMES: I don't know, honey, I think you still have this fantasy
that one day he's going to turn into a really great guy.

MANDY: Well, *I* think your wedding was just right. *(To Richard)* I wish *we* had done it like this.

RICHARD: I liked what we did . . .

MANDY: A few close friends, finger food, cake and champagne? Perfect.

SARAH: *Your* wedding was wonderful.

MANDY: Yeah? But it wasn't *me*; it was all my mother. I let her do whatever she wanted; it just wasn't worth it. She didn't freak out when I told her I was pregnant but when I said I didn't want to have a big wedding . . . she was like, "You are too having a big wedding! We didn't hold on to the house in Vermont all these years to *not* have a big wedding there!" *(A beat)* I'm sorry about the hors d'oeuvres.

SARAH: Why? What was wrong with them?

MANDY: They sucked. *(Shows discarded plates)* See? Nobody ate them.

RICHARD: I did. The scallops wrapped in bacon . . . They were fantastic; I ate too many of them.

SARAH: Oh, yeah, those were good.

MANDY: I liked them, too, even though I shouldn't be eating them.

SARAH: Why not?

MANDY: Mollusks. Any kind of shellfish. I was bad: I had *one*. *(To Richard)* One little scallop's not gonna hurt, right?

RICHARD: Honey, you've been so good . . .

MANDY: What did you think of the little quiches?

SARAH: Those . . . ? Not so good.

RICHARD: No.

MANDY: I know! They tasted like soap. We use this caterer a *lot*. I don't know what happened.

RICHARD: So they had an off night . . .

MANDY: Naturally it had to be *your* wedding. Oh God.

SARAH: Don't worry about it, it was fine. You did a great job of setting all this up.

MANDY: Yeah?

RICHARD: Didn't she?

SARAH: We really appreciate it. Thank you.

MANDY: Don't mention it. I'm glad I could be useful.

SARAH: See? All that event planning paid off.

MANDY: You think?

SARAH: What are you doing about your job?

MANDY: Work till the baby comes, or till I start bumping into things, then I'll take off like a month or so. *(An idea)* Wouldn't it be awesome if we had babies together?!

SARAH: That's a very big "if" . . .

MANDY: Why?

SARAH: I'm not sure I still can.

MANDY: I'm sure you can.

SARAH: *I'm* not; I'm *old.*

MANDY: You're not old.

SARAH: Yes. I *am.*

MANDY: My OBGYN is fantastic; I bet she knows a really good fertility guy. I can ask . . .

SARAH: That's okay.

MANDY: Maybe when we have our second, you'll have your first!

RICHARD *(Changing the subject)*: I'd like to make a toast. *(A beat)* What I *didn't* say earlier, and wish I had . . . *(Emotional; stops to compose himself)* I'm losing it already.

SARAH *(Affectionately)*: Oh, Richard . . .

RICHARD *(A deep breath; then)*: There are certain people in your life who you not only love, you admire. Who lead exemplary—if not always supportable—lives.

(They laugh.)

Sarah and Jamie? *(His voice cracks)* You're my golden couple.

JAMES: Aw . . .

MANDY: He's gotten so emotional lately. I think it's the baby.

RICHARD: I've lived vicariously through you for years; I got to see the world without jet lag. *(Sarah and James chuckle. He raises his glass)* To Sarah and Jamie: no longer living in sin. And it's about fucking time!

JAMES: Hear, hear.

(They drink.)

SARAH: Thank you, Richard.

RICHARD *(Remembers)*: Got something for you.

JAMES: We said, no gifts, remember?

RICHARD *(Getting a gift-wrapped book)*: Just a little something. *(Refers to the flat-screen TV)* Where'd *this* baby come from?

JAMES: Present. From me to me.

(Richard hands his gift to Sarah.)

SARAH *(Parodying a Southern bride)*: Why, the wrapping paper's so pretty, I hate to rip it. *(She tears it open)* Oh, nice!

JAMES: What.

SARAH: *Slightly Out of Focus.* Robert Capa.

RICHARD: First edition. 1947.

JAMES: Oh, great. You know, I've never read it.

SARAH *(Embarrassed)*: Neither have I.

RICHARD: It's a treat, it really is.

SARAH: Perfect gift, Richard, thank you.

RICHARD: From both of us, actually.

SARAH: Of course . . .

MANDY: I wrapped it.

SARAH: Thank you, Mandy.

MANDY: You're welcome.

SARAH: Great wrapping.

RICHARD: Capa plays pretty fast and loose with the truth, by the way. He was looking to sell his story to the movies.

JAMES: Did he?

RICHARD: Never happened. The D-day story is true, though. The kid in the darkroom *did* ruin most of the negatives.

MANDY: Why, what happened?

RICHARD: He was so anxious for them to dry, he turned up the heat on the dryer.

MANDY: Oh my God, you're kidding.

SARAH: Famous boo-boo.

RICHARD: How's *our* book coming?

JAMES *(Equivocally)*: It's coming . . .

RICHARD: When do I get to see what you've written?

JAMES: Soon.

RICHARD *(To Sarah)*: Have *you* seen it?

SARAH: Not *me* . . .

JAMES: It's not like I haven't been working on it; I *have* been.

RICHARD: I know you guys have had a lot on your minds . . .

SARAH: Don't look at *me*; my work is done.

RICHARD *(To James)*: I've stayed out of your way. Haven't I?

JAMES: Yes, Richard.

RICHARD: Gave you plenty of time to get it together. Well, now I'm cracking the whip. What else do you have on your plate right now?

JAMES: I'm expanding that horror-movie piece I did into a book.

MANDY: Oh, cool.

RICHARD: Well, too bad! Ours should be in first position.

JAMES: It is! I go back and forth between the two.

RICHARD: No more screwing around . . .

JAMES: I'm not screwing around.

RICHARD: I need it by the end of the week.

JAMES: What?!

RICHARD: Or we're going to miss the spring list! Read the Capa book; maybe it'll inspire you.

JAMES: Oh, *I* get it . . . What a subtle guy! Hey, whatever happened to my refugee piece?

(James unsteadily refills his glass.)

SARAH *(Sotto voce)*: That's enough.

(She tries to take away the bottle from James; he takes it back.)

JAMES: It's my wedding day!

SARAH: It's *my* wedding day, too, and I'd appreciate it if the groom wasn't shit-faced.

(James surrenders the bottle.)

RICHARD: Sarah, let me ask you something: Do you think you're ready to go back to work?

(Sarah and James look at one another.)

SARAH: Well, I don't know, depends on what you have in mind.

RICHARD: There's an open assignment I thought you'd be right for.

SARAH: What is it?

RICHARD: We're doing a piece on a day-care center at a women's prison. We need someone to shoot it.

MANDY: Oh, wow.

RICHARD: You're the first person I thought of; everybody *loved* the idea. *(To James)* The story's already been assigned or else I would've uh . . .

SARAH: When would you need it?

RICHARD: As soon as possible. Sometime this week.

SARAH: This week!

RICHARD: I know it's such short notice. This literally came up the other night.

JAMES *(This topic makes him uneasy)*: Are you up for it?

SARAH *(To Richard)*: Where is it?

RICHARD: Not far. Two hours at most, depending on traffic. You could easily do it in a day.

SARAH: *Getting* there might be a bit of a challenge.

JAMES: I could get you there. We'll rent a car.

RICHARD: *I'll* get her there. I'll hire a car to bring her up and take her back.

JAMES: She's still a little shaky; I don't know how I feel about her taking off on her own like that.

RICHARD: If she wants an assistant, we'll send an intern.

SARAH: Jesus! Would you two stop talking about me as if I weren't here?!

JAMES: Sorry.

RICHARD: It's a good fit for you; just the sort of story you *should* be doing. There are great stories right here, you know, right outside your door.

SARAH: Oh, so this is part of your Keep Sarah Home initiative.

RICHARD *(Shrugs)*: Sue me.

SARAH: Well, maybe it would help me get my sea legs back.

JAMES: What if you fell? What if you reinjured yourself?

SARAH: I'm not going to fall . . .

JAMES: How do you know? That would feel pretty stupid, wouldn't it, after all the progress we've made.

SARAH: I was just on the stairs all by myself, and I did fine . . .

JAMES: You're *familiar* with these stairs; we've been practicing . . .

RICHARD: Look, just think about it. Okay? You don't have to tell me right this minute.

SARAH: I don't need to think about it. I want to do it.

RICHARD: Great. That's wonderful. Everybody'll be thrilled.

JAMES *(Sarcastic, to Richard)*: Thanks a lot.

RICHARD: What.

JAMES: She isn't ready!

SARAH: I can do it; I want to give it a try.

JAMES: It's too much, too soon!

RICHARD: Think of it as part of her rehab.

JAMES: What do you know about rehab? It could be dangerous, going out too soon!

RICHARD: I'm talking about Westchester!

SARAH: Come on, Jamie, you're overreacting.

JAMES *(Emotionally)*: If anything happens to her . . . !

SARAH *(Facetiously)*: Honey, you're getting maudlin.

JAMES *(Feeling patronized, he pulls away; to Richard)*: So are you ever going to tell me what the deal is with my refugee piece?

RICHARD: What?

JAMES: Did you think I forgot about it?

RICHARD: No . . .

JAMES: Does it have a date yet or what?

RICHARD: Look, let's not talk business. Okay? My mistake. I should never have—

JAMES: It's not going to run, is it.

RICHARD: Jamie, let's not get into this. Okay?

JAMES: Fuck. How long have you known?

RICHARD: A week or so.

JAMES: A *week*?! *(To Sarah)* Did you know?

SARAH: No.

JAMES *(To Richard)*: When were you planning on telling me?

RICHARD: You were getting married, for Christ's sake! I didn't want to spoil things. I knew how much it meant to you.

SARAH: That was a great piece.

RICHARD: It was, I know.

SARAH: One of the best things he's ever written.

RICHARD: Absolutely.

JAMES *(Sarcastic)*: Thanks.

RICHARD: Everyone agreed: it was an excellent, excellent piece.

JAMES: So you killed it? Are you in the habit of killing excellent stories?

RICHARD: It wasn't my decision. It was an editorial decision.

JAMES: Yeah, right.

SARAH: Take it elsewhere. The *Atlantic*, or *Harper's* . . .

JAMES: It's too late.

RICHARD: Don't worry, you'll get your full fee.

JAMES: I don't give a shit about my fee!

SARAH: What happened?

RICHARD: The usual bullshit. Scheduling. It was just a matter of timing.

JAMES: They've had it for months!

RICHARD: I know.

JAMES: They've been *sitting on it* for months!

RICHARD: That was part of the problem: its shelf life expired.

JAMES: Whose fault was that?!

SARAH: Jamie . . .

RICHARD: It was *on* the board, then it was *off* . . . Then they wanted to cut it . . .

JAMES: Cut it?! I already cut fifteen hundred words!

RICHARD: I knew you would have a fit, so I got them to leave the length alone and bump it a week. Then it had to get bumped *three* weeks, 'cause the week after *that* was a special issue.

JAMES: What special issue?

RICHARD *(Hesitates)*: The annual Hollywood issue.

JAMES *(To Sarah)*: The Hollywood issue.

RICHARD: That's a big one for us. All the movie studios buy a shitload of advertising space. *(James laughs)* Don't laugh; the ad revenue for that one issue helps us stay afloat all year. But then we realized your story *couldn't* run the week after that . . .

JAMES: Why not?

RICHARD *(Hesitates)*: 'Cause we'd already committed to a cover story on relief workers in Africa.

(A beat.)

JAMES: You're kidding me.

RICHARD: Come on . . . you know how it works.

JAMES: You can't have relief workers in Africa and Iraqi refugees in the same issue? What is there, *a quota*?!

RICHARD: It wasn't my call!

JAMES: Bullshit. You sold me out!

SARAH: Jamie . . .

JAMES *(To Sarah)*: We go to these fucking hellholes . . . put our lives on the line . . . For what? Stories that nobody wants?

SARAH: It's not true nobody wants them.

JAMES: It's true for *me* . . . You're a star; somebody will always publish your pictures. Me, I peddle stories around like a traveling salesman! Pieces get killed, or cut to shreds.

RICHARD: Editorial has the final say what goes in the magazine, not me!

JAMES: You were in the room! Sitting there!

RICHARD: I'm only the photo editor, for Christ's sake! The only reason *I'm* telling you, is 'cause you're my friend.

JAMES: Oh, I see.

RICHARD: I didn't want you hearing about it from someone else.

JAMES: Well, thanks a lot, *buddy*.

RICHARD: Listen: I fight at work every fucking day! Every fucking day is another battle! I go into these staff meetings . . . everybody's got their own agenda! The fashion people, the style people . . . We're all fighting for the same goddamn space. Somewhere in there, between the ads for imported silk lingerie and twenty-million-dollar condos, *maybe* I'll get four pages on boy mercenaries in Uganda. Six if I'm lucky. So don't tell me how I sold you out.

JAMES: You talk out of both sides of your mouth, you know that?!

SARAH: James.

JAMES: You're the reporter's advocate one minute; one of Them the next!

RICHARD: Jamie, come on, that's not fair.

JAMES: Who are you really? Huh? My friend? Or just another "suit"?!

MANDY: Stop it!

(They look at her.)

Richard *agonized* over this!

RICHARD: Honey . . .

MANDY: He was sick about it! For days! He couldn't sleep! He *loves* you. Why would he want to hurt you? I mean, really. He's only doing his job. They have a magazine to put out. And it has to have different things *in* it, not just stories about how *miserable* most of the world is. So they're not going to print your story—too bad. They've already got a "bummer" story running that week.

JAMES: Excuse me?

MANDY: No, I mean it, I'm really sorry, I bet you worked really hard on it.

JAMES: What the fuck do you know?

RICHARD: Hey.

JAMES: Hundreds of thousands of lives are at stake. That's why I write these fucking things. People need to know.

MANDY: But what am I supposed to do with this information? Me: an ordinary person. It's not like I can *do* anything. Besides feel bad, and turn the page, and thank God I was born in the half of the world where people have food to eat and don't go around hacking each other to death. The people who are killing each other have always been killing each other, and terrible things are always going to happen, so . . .

JAMES: You can stop whining and *do* something for crissake!

RICHARD: All right that's enough.

JAMES: Don't just throw your hands up and say, *(Mocking)* "Oh, dear. What can *I* do? Little me. I'm powerless; I can't do *any*thing."

SARAH: James.

(Sarah reaches out to James. He brusquely pulls away, throwing her off balance. Mandy gasps. Silence.)

RICHARD *(To Sarah)*: I'll call you tomorrow.

(Richard gets his and Mandy's things. Silence. Mandy turns before she goes.)

MANDY: You know what I wish? There's so much beauty in the world. But you only see misery. Both of you. I wish you'd just let yourselves feel the *joy*. Y'know? *(A beat)* Otherwise . . . what's the point?

(Richard and Mandy leave. Sarah looks at James.)

2.

A few days later. Late afternoon. Rain. James is watching a horror movie like Friday the 13th *while taking notes on his laptop. Sarah, camera bags in hand, comes in from the rain.*

JAMES: Hey!
SARAH: Hey.

(He turns off the TV.)

JAMES: Why didn't your little intern help you up with this?
SARAH: I sent her home.
JAMES: You should've buzzed me; I would have come down.
SARAH: I could manage.
JAMES: How'd it go?
SARAH: Fine.
JAMES: You get some good stuff?
SARAH: Yeah.
JAMES: So . . . ?
SARAH: Let me catch my breath.
JAMES: Want something? Tea or uh . . .

SARAH: Something harder would be great.

JAMES: Got it. *(He pours glasses of scotch. As he hands one to her)* So tell me!

SARAH: It's not such a big deal.

JAMES: It *is* a big deal. Your first assignment in six months? That's a very big deal.

SARAH: How was *your* day?

JAMES: You're looking at it.

SARAH: What're you cooking?

JAMES: That chicken—black olive thing.

SARAH: Again?

JAMES: Thought I'd try not to make it rare this time.

SARAH *(Regarding his laptop)*: What are you working on?

JAMES: My horror movie book.

SARAH: What about the pages for Richard? You promised he'd have it on Friday.

JAMES: I know; he will.

SARAH: You can't blow it off; you've got to do it.

JAMES: I am! I worked on it all day. Now I'm working on *this*.

SARAH: When can I read it?

JAMES: Soon. *(A beat)* You okay? You seem wrecked.

SARAH: Long day.

JAMES: It was too much for you wasn't it? I knew it would be too much.

SARAH: It wasn't that.

JAMES: Didn't I say you weren't ready?

SARAH: Physically I held up just fine. *(Pause)* I had a flash-back.

(Pause.)

JAMES: At the prison? *(She nods)* What was it?

SARAH: Market bombing. Mosul. Couple of years ago.

JAMES: What happened today? What was the trigger?

(Pause.)

SARAH (*A deep breath*): Today . . . I'm shooting these women.
The inmates. With the babies they'd had in prison.

JAMES: Yeah . . .

SARAH: And *some* of these ladies are *seriously* bad. I mean:
homicide, drug dealing, trying to kill their grand-
mother for her ATM card, that kind of thing . . .
Anyway I'm shooting . . . sort of getting in the zone and
this one woman . . . big . . . heavily tattooed with Hell's
Angels' kind of skulls with fire coming out of the eye
sockets, comes up to me, gets right in my face . . . and
looks at me with such . . . contempt . . . (*Brutish voice*)
"What you want to take my picture for? Huh?" And . . . I
was back in Mosul.

JAMES: Was I with you?

SARAH: You were off doing a story in the south; it was when
I was there for the AP.

JAMES: What happened that day? I don't remember.

SARAH: That's because I never told you. I never told anybody.

JAMES: Tell me now. (*She shakes her head. Gently*) Come on.
Tell me.

(*Pause.*)

SARAH: The light that day was gorgeous, I remember. (*Pause*)
I was sitting in a café with the Reuters guys . . . And a
car bomb went off, a block or two away, in this market.
And I just *ran* to it, took off. Without even thinking.

(*A beat.*)

The carnage was . . . ridiculous. Exploded produce.
Body parts. Eggplants. Women keening. They were
digging in the rubble for their children. I started shooting. And suddenly this woman burst out from the
smoke . . . covered in blood . . . her skin was raw and red
and charred, and her hair was singed—she got so close

I could smell it—and her clothes, her top had melted into her, and she was screaming at me. *(Shouts)* "Go way, go way! No picture, no picture!" And she started pushing me, pushing my camera with her hand on the lens . . .

JAMES: What did you do?

SARAH: Nothing. I kept on shooting. Then, somehow, I ran the hell out of there. I stopped to catch my breath . . . and check out my cameras . . . *(Pause)* There was blood on my lens. *(Moved)* Her blood was smeared on my lens. *(She breaks down)* I feel so ashamed . . .

JAMES: No! Why?

SARAH: It was wrong . . . What I did was so wrong.

JAMES: It wasn't wrong.

SARAH: It was indecent.

JAMES: You were doing your job.

SARAH: They didn't want me there! They didn't want me taking pictures! They lost *children* in that mess! To them it was a sacred place. But there I was, like a, like a *ghoul* with a camera, shooting away. No wonder they wanted to kill me; I would've wanted to kill me, too.

JAMES *(Soothing)*: No . . .

SARAH: I live off the suffering of strangers. I built a *career* on the sorrows of people I don't know and will never see again.

JAMES: That's not true. You've helped them. In ways you can't see.

SARAH: Have I? Have I really? *(Pause)* I'm such a fraud.

(Long pause.)

JAMES: Hey. *(She looks at him. Pause)* We *don't* have to do this anymore, you know.

SARAH: What do you mean?

JAMES: We don't have to *do* this. We can stay home. We can *make* a home.

(A beat.)

Y'know? The past few months? Teaching myself how to cook, watching Netflix . . . writing while you napped, listening to you breathe . . . I've been so . . . *(Chokes up)* *happy.* Y'know? Simple, boring, happy. *(A beat)* For the first time in I don't know how long, I don't have giardia, or some nasty parasite I'm trying to get rid of . . . And my back doesn't ache from sleeping on the ground, or on lousy mattresses in shitty hotels. I realized: Wow, this is what it must feel like to be *comfortable.* I don't think I've ever known that feeling; maybe as a boy I did, I felt safe, but I didn't know what it was. Now I know! I just want to be comfortable! There! I said it! Does that make me a bad person?

SARAH: Of course not.

JAMES: I've been feeling like, we're going *back* there? *Why?* Unfinished business? Fuck unfinished business. I don't need to dodge bullets to feel alive anymore. Or step over mutilated corpses. Or watch children die. I want to watch children *grow.* And take vacations like other people. To . . . I don't know, *dude* ranches. Or Club Med. I don't want to be on a goddamn mission every time I get on a plane! I want to take our kids to Disney World and buy them all the crap they want.

SARAH: Our kids.

JAMES *(Nods, then)*: Let's just do it. We keep putting it off, and putting it off. We're pushing our luck already. Let's just go ahead and do it. Now. Not six months from now. *(Pause)* There'll always be something, some reason to put our lives on hold. The war *du jour.* Well, fuck it. It's our turn now. *(A beat)* Let's stop running.

3.

Later that night. The rain has stopped. James, lit only by the TV, reclines on the sofa, watching Invasion of the Body Snatchers. *The volume is low. Unseen by him, Sarah is sitting up in bed with his computer on her lap, illuminated by its screen. She gets up purposefully and pauses in the dark to see what he is watching.*

JAMES *(Startled)*: Whoa! Didn't see you. What are you looking for?

SARAH: Gotta be a cigarette around here *somewhere . . .*

JAMES: What do you want a cigarette for?

SARAH: I want to smoke it.

JAMES: Don't. You haven't had a cigarette in months.

SARAH: I want one now . . .

(He watches her look through drawers, pockets, etc.)

JAMES: I thought you were sleeping.

SARAH: Never got there.

JAMES: If this was keeping you up . . . You should've told me . . . I would've made it lower.

SARAH: What *is* this? *(Meaning: "on TV.")*

JAMES: *Invasion of the Body Snatchers.* The original. 1956. Research. Come sit down.

(He makes room. She ignores the gesture.)

SARAH: Why do you watch this shit?

JAMES: What?

SARAH: Why do you *watch* this shit.

JAMES: This isn't shit . . .

SARAH *(Looks at Netflix envelopes)*: *Saw II . . . Saw IV . . .*

JAMES: It's an allegory for the McCarthy era. All about the Red Scare.

(She continues looking.)

Honey, there *are* no cigarettes.

SARAH: This is your idea of escapism? Replacing real horror with fake horror?

JAMES: Yes. Exactly. It gets me out of my head. So, yeah; whatever it takes. *(A beat)* Look, I know you think movies are a waste of time.

SARAH: That's not true.

JAMES: You've *always* thought movies were a waste of time.

SARAH: I think *most* movies are a waste of time. I think writing about *shitty* movies is certainly a waste of *your* time, legi*ti*mizing crap like this . . .

(She rummages through her camera bag, finds a lone, broken cigarette, then searches for a match.)

JAMES: Look, what the fuck are you so . . . ? I said I was sorry I woke you.

SARAH: You didn't wake me. I was up. Reading.

JAMES: What were you reading?

SARAH: The thing you wrote. For our book.

(She smokes the cigarette. Pause.)

JAMES: How did you uh . . . ?

SARAH: It was on your laptop.

JAMES: What were you doing on my laptop?

SARAH: It was on the bed! I couldn't sleep 'cause of all the screaming coming from your fucking movie . . .

JAMES: I *said*, if it was too loud, you should have *said* something.

SARAH: . . . so I thought I'd go online.

JAMES: You went poking around my laptop?

SARAH: "Poking around"? I opened it up! There it was! Right on the screen! If you didn't want me to see it, why'd you leave it up?

(Pause.)

JAMES: How much did you read?

SARAH: The whole thing.

JAMES: It's not finished.

SARAH: Bullshit.

JAMES: I'm still working on it

SARAH: Isn't Richard expecting it *tomorrow*?

JAMES: Yeah, but I . . .

SARAH: Then it's finished.

JAMES: I was going to give it another pass in the morning.

SARAH: Were you ever going to let me see it?

JAMES: Yes. In the morning. *(Sarah scoffs)* This was hard, Sare. You *have* your pictures. You can *hold* them, and move them around. I had to replay everything in my head so I could write about it. I needed to process it on my own.

SARAH: "Process it"? You mean like put it through a blender? Pulverize it?

JAMES: I needed to make sense of it. Okay?

SARAH: Was erasing history part of your process?

JAMES: What?

SARAH: How could you do that to him? After all that man went through . . . !

JAMES: What are you talking about?

SARAH: Tariq. How could you annihilate him all over again?!

JAMES: "Annihilate" him? How did I "annihilate" him?

SARAH: You wrote him out of our story! Deleted him! Like he never existed!

JAMES: No, I didn't.

SARAH: Like in the old Politburo days: they'd white-out the undesirables till there was no one left in the picture!

JAMES: He's there . . . I mention him . . .

SARAH: Mention! Yeah! In passing! Like the scenery!

JAMES: He's not what interested me.

SARAH *(Incredulous)*: He's not?!

JAMES: Not primarily, no.

SARAH: My God! And you call yourself a journalist?! *He's* the story! The indignity that man endured! His entire life! And still had such humanity! Such grace!

JAMES: Christ, you make him sound like a saint!

SARAH: Maybe he was! Maybe he's what being a saint is really about!

JAMES: You mean fucking other men's women?

SARAH: Is that what I am? *(Mock macho)* Your "woman"?

JAMES: He was a scrappy opportunist just like everybody else you meet over there.

SARAH: You just can't bear the thought that he and I were lovers, can you?

JAMES: Don't say "lovers."

SARAH: So what do you do? Delete him! Poof! He's gone!

JAMES: You know what *I* think? I don't even think it was Tariq you fell in love with.

SARAH: Oh, no?

JAMES: No. It was his suffering. His victimhood. The romance of his wretched people. Holy cow! What a turn on! You were fucking Oppression itself!

SARAH: That's a shitty thing to say.

JAMES: If he'd been just another brown-skinned New York cabbie, you wouldn't've looked twice at him in the rearview mirror!

SARAH: If I'd met *you* in the bar on the corner who's to say I would have looked twice at *you*?

JAMES: At least you and I had things in common! We knew where each other was coming from . . .

SARAH: You think that's all it takes, having things in common?

JAMES: *Some* kind of common ground. *Something.* His *English* wasn't even that good.

SARAH: His English was *very* good!

JAMES: He wasn't even that good a translator.

SARAH: You know, you're beginning to sound like some fucking imperialist!

JAMES: "Imperialist"?!

SARAH: Yes! There's a hint—more than a hint—of racism here, you know that?

JAMES: Oh, really, and your fascination with his exoticism, that isn't a kind of racism? Gunga Din? The "noble savage"?

SARAH: Fuck you! *(A beat) Fuck* you.

(Long pause.)

JAMES: Sarah . . . *(Pause)* Can't we just . . . ? The hell with it. The hell with all of it. I want us to move on now. Can we? Please?

(Long pause.)

SARAH: I can't.

JAMES: Oh God, is he going to haunt us the rest of our lives?

SARAH: I'm not talking about Tariq. *(Pause)* I'm talking about this.

JAMES: What.

SARAH: This life you want. I can't do it; I thought I could but I can't.

JAMES: Wait a minute wait a minute. This life *I* want? What do you mean this life *I* want? If I remember correctly, we just got married. *(She says nothing)* Hello?

(Pause.)

SARAH: I could never have gotten through this without you. *(He scoffs)* I mean it. I'll always be grateful.

JAMES: Fuck that.

SARAH: What.

JAMES: "Grateful." I don't want you to be "grateful."

SARAH: Why not? You didn't have to take this on; you could've walked away.

JAMES: No, I couldn't have. I did what a person does. That's all. It's what you *do*. *(A beat)* Is that why you married me? Because you were grateful?

SARAH: You wanted it so much . . .

JAMES: Oh, for fuck's sake . . .

SARAH: And I wanted so much to make you happy . . .

JAMES: I don't believe this . . .

SARAH: I thought marriage would change me. If I said and did all the right things . . . I would *feel* it; it would be so. But . . . *(She shakes her head)*

(Pause.)

JAMES: So, having kids . . . ? That was just . . . ? *(She averts his eyes)* Jesus . . .

SARAH: Do you see me pushing a stroller and going to play-dates? Honestly, Jamie, do you?

JAMES: You said you were ready, remember?

SARAH: I thought I was!

JAMES: You fucking lied to me!

SARAH: I did not lie to you! If I lied to you, I lied to myself!

(Silence.)

I'm not what you want anymore.

JAMES: Don't tell me what I want.

SARAH: You want a playmate. That isn't me . . . You want a Mandy.

JAMES: That is not what I want.

SARAH: Someone young, who adores you, and will give you all the babies you want. You should have the life you want.

JAMES: All I want . . . All I *ever* wanted . . . is a life with you.

SARAH: I wish I could kick back and watch movies with you, I really do. But I can't. There's too much going on. I can't sit still.

JAMES: What am I supposed to do? Pack you off to hell whenever you need your adrenaline-fix, and hope you'll come home in one piece? Is that what you expect me to do?

SARAH: I don't expect you to do anything. I'm telling you I can't *do* this.

(Pause.)

(Posing a question) You've seen the things I've seen . . .

JAMES: Yeah . . . ?

SARAH: How can you live with yourself, knowing what goes on out there?

JAMES: How? *Because* I know what goes on out there—and on, and on—whether you and I are there to cover it or not. *(Pause)* So you actually believe what you do can change anything.

SARAH: It's got to.

(Silence. He smiles to himself, shakes his head ironically.)

What. *(He makes a dismissive gesture)* What were you thinking?

JAMES: You'll laugh at me.
SARAH: No I won't.

(A beat.)

JAMES: *Days of Wine and Roses.* Blake Edwards. 1962. Jack
Lemmon, Lee Remick, drinking themselves into obliv-
ion; he hits the wall, goes on the wagon, but she . . . can't
do it. She needs the buzz more than she needs him.

(A beat.)

Well, here I am: Jack Lemmon on the wagon. But
you . . .
SARAH: I'm a drunk?
JAMES: You need it. The whole fucking mess of it. The chaos,
and the drama. You need it. *(A beat)* More than you
need me.
SARAH: Not more than I need you.

(They sit in silence. He nods.)

4.

Four months later. Late afternoon. A bicycle stands near the door. Mandy nurses her infant nestled in a sling. Richard and James stand over Sarah who looks at their published book.

SARAH: That's good.
RICHARD: Yeah, I thought the juxtaposition . . .
SARAH *(Turns the page; annoyed)*: These two-page spreads . . . !
JAMES: I know.
RICHARD: Here we go . . . *(Meaning: he's heard this before)*
SARAH: Look at that, Richard, it looks horrible.
RICHARD: It does not look horrible.
SARAH: Look how much you lose! You can never see the whole image!
JAMES: Unless you split the binding.
SARAH: Exactly.
RICHARD: I assure you it doesn't bother anyone nearly as much as it bothers you.
SARAH: I doubt that very much.
RICHARD: It's a picture book! People understand that.
SARAH *(To James)*: This is one battle I was never going to win.

RICHARD: You're unbelievable.

SARAH: It looks beautiful, Richard. Congratulations.

RICHARD: Congratulations to *you*. You guys made it happen.

SARAH: We never would have done it without *you*.

JAMES: I still don't know who's gonna rush out to *buy* it.

RICHARD: Plenty of people.

JAMES: To put on their coffee tables? For guests to flip through over cocktails? "Oh, darling, look at these marvelous atrocities. Pass the crudités?"

(They laugh. Sarah lights a cigarette.)

MANDY: Could you not smoke?

SARAH: What? Oh. Okay . . .

(Sarah puts out her cigarette.)

MANDY: Thanks. It's just, I don't want the baby . . .

SARAH: No no, I understand.

RICHARD: Ever since the baby was born, Mandy's gotten super sensitive about this stuff.

MANDY *(Not harshly)*: You don't have to speak for me . . . I can speak for myself . . .

RICHARD *(Sheepish)*: Sorry, I was just . . .

MANDY *(To Sarah)*: I felt it the first time I held her: this amazing feeling. You become like hyper-aware of everything. You don't know, you *can't* know what it's like till it's *your* child you're holding.

RICHARD: Man . . .

MANDY *(To Richard)*: Should I not have said that?

SARAH: No, you can say it.

MANDY: You realize . . . your life will never be the same. You'll always have this feeling . . . in your chest . . . like a . . . sigh you can never let out. This fear . . . that something could happen to her. You just want to hold on to her forever.

SARAH: Which of course you can't.

MANDY: I know.

SARAH: You're going to have to send her to school one day . . .

MANDY: I've thought about that. I was thinking maybe I'll home-school her.

RICHARD *(News to him)*: Really?

MANDY: Maybe.

RICHARD: Huh.

SARAH: When do you go back to work?

MANDY: I'm not.

SARAH: No?

RICHARD: Yeah, she decided she doesn't want to— *(Stops himself; to Mandy)* Sorry.

MANDY: I was supposed to go back in like three weeks? But the closer it got, I found myself feeling sadder and sadder. I was crying *all the time. (To Richard)* Wasn't I? *(He nods)* Just the thought of turning her over to someone else . . . A stranger. It didn't seem natural. Who could possibly love her more than I do?

RICHARD: *I'm* pretty crazy about her . . .

MANDY: Of course you are. I mean, it's not like I do something *important* . . . Why would I do something like totally trivial when I could be home raising my child?

SARAH: Makes sense.

MANDY: You mean that?

SARAH: Yes. Why?

MANDY: I don't know, somehow I'm made to feel like there's something wrong with me, like I must not be a serious woman, because I want to stay home and raise my child.

SARAH: Who makes you feel that way?

MANDY: Well, *you* do.

SARAH: I do?

MANDY: Maybe you're not even aware of doing it? But sometimes you . . .

RICHARD *(To Mandy)*: Honey, y'know?, I think it's time we uh . . .

SARAH: Thanks for bringing the book.

RICHARD: Don't mention it. Wanted to make sure you got to see it before you left.

SARAH: Well, thanks for stopping by.

RICHARD: Bye, darlin'. *(Hugs Sarah)*

SARAH: Bye.

RICHARD: Send me great stuff.

SARAH: I will.

RICHARD: And if you need anything, promise me you'll call me!

SARAH: I promise.

(Richard has his arm around Mandy and their baby. A beat.)

RICHARD: Be happy.

SARAH: I *am* happy. This is me happy.

RICHARD *(Nods; then to James)*: You I'll see later.

JAMES: Bye!

MANDY *(To Sarah)*: I can't believe she slept the whole time; I was hoping you'd get to see all the neat tricks she does.

SARAH: I will. Next time I see her, she'll have a whole new repertoire. *(Admires the baby for the first time and is moved. A beat)* She's beautiful.

MANDY: Isn't she? She's an angel.

SARAH: Yeah. She is.

MANDY: Well . . . Bye.

SARAH: Bye.

(They hug.)

MANDY: Can we email each other?

SARAH: Of course.

MANDY: I'll send you pictures. Of her, I mean.

SARAH: Do that.

MANDY *(To James)*: Are you uh . . . ? *(Meaning: "coming with us?")*

JAMES: No, I'm uh . . . *(Meaning: "staying.")*
MANDY: Oh, right.
RICHARD: Safe journey, kiddo.
MANDY: Have a great trip.
JAMES *(Calling to them as they leave)*: See ya.

(Sarah closes the door. She and James are alone. Pause.)

SARAH: She seems . . . *(Meaning: "different.")*
JAMES: I know. She's actually a wonderful mother.
SARAH: I bet.
JAMES: She's found her calling.

(She smiles, nods. A beat.)

SARAH: So, what have you been up to?
JAMES: Not much. I've got some freelance gigs lined up. A
    long piece for *Vanity Fair* . . .
SARAH: Oh, good! What?
JAMES: A celebrity profile. I'm not even gonna tell you of
    whom; you'll only give me shit for it.

(Pause.)

So, what's your first stop?
SARAH: Kabul. Then, on to Kandahar. Then, we'll see . . .
    You're welcome to *stay* here, you know.
JAMES: What do you mean?
SARAH: While I'm gone.
JAMES: Oh no I uh . . .
SARAH: Are you sure?
JAMES: Positive.
SARAH: I'll be gone two months at least.
JAMES: I know.
SARAH: You'll have it all to yourself.

83

JAMES: I couldn't. Be way too weird. Thanks, though. I'll
probably come by sometime for the rest of my books
and stuff.

SARAH: Sure.

JAMES: *And* the TV.

SARAH: It's all yours. *(A beat)* Sleeping on Richard's couch
can't be as comfy as all that . . .

JAMES: Actually, I'm uh . . . there's a good chance I'll be moving out pretty soon.

SARAH: You found something?

JAMES: It's someone else's. *All* the way uptown. Near the
hospital.

SARAH: Whose?

JAMES: I'm seeing this person, actually.

(A beat.)

SARAH: Oh! Wow! *(He nods)* Good for you!

JAMES: Yeah, thanks. Been a couple of months now. She asked
me if I wanted to move in and I uh . . .

SARAH: So it's serious.

JAMES: I think it *is*, yeah.

(A beat.)

SARAH: I'm afraid to ask: Is she a grown-up?

JAMES: Forty-one.

SARAH: Wow!

JAMES: Her name is Visna.

SARAH: Indian?

JAMES: Cambodian.

SARAH: Ah.

JAMES: She's an ER doc. Came over when she was around ten.
Divorced. One kid. A son.

SARAH: A son.

JAMES: Twelve years old. Great kid. He's a riot, actually.

SARAH: Yeah?

JAMES: He really is. I love 'im. We have a lot of fun.

SARAH: Instant family.

JAMES: Yeah.

SARAH: See that? *That* didn't take very long, did it.

(He smiles. Silence.)

JAMES: What about you? Are *you*, uh . . . ? *(Meaning: "seeing anyone?")*

SARAH: Nah . . .

(Silence.)

JAMES: I should let you pack.

SARAH: Just my usual quart of Imodium and vat of sunscreen.

JAMES: What time's your flight?

SARAH: I'm okay. I don't have to be at the airport till eight or nine.

JAMES: I promised I would stay with the baby tonight so they could go out to eat.

SARAH: Aren't *you* the hands-on uncle!

JAMES: It's the least I can do to earn my keep.

SARAH: Better go then.

JAMES *(Nods, then)*: Well . . . Take care of yourself.

SARAH: You, too.

JAMES: Have a safe trip.

SARAH: Thank you.

JAMES: Write to me.

SARAH: I will.

JAMES: And I'll write to you.

(She nods. Pause. He tentatively opens his arms. She hesitates before entering his embrace. They hug fervently for a very long time, neither one wishing to be the one who breaks it. Finally Sarah gently separates from him.)

SARAH: Thanks again for bringing over the book.
JAMES: Wait, I wanted to . . . You didn't see this . . .

(He finds a place in the text. She reads silently and is moved.)

SARAH: Nice, Jamie. That's nice.
JAMES: I took another crack at it.
SARAH: It's good. I'm glad you did.

(Pause. He dons his bike helmet.)

JAMES: Well . . . Happy trails.
SARAH: Happy trails.

(He carries his bike out the door. She watches him go down the stairs.)

(Calling) Careful.

(Sarah shuts the door, takes a deep breath, and begins to pack her cameras. She polishes a lens, gets lost in thought for a moment, then attaches the lens to a camera. She looks out and sees something in the distance. Just as she is about to take a picture, the lights quickly fade to black.)

END OF PLAY

DONALD MARGULIES received the 2000 Pulitzer Prize for Drama for *Dinner with Friends* (Variety Arts Theatre, New York; Comedie des Champs-Elysées, Paris; Hampstead Theatre, London; Actors Theatre of Louisville; South Coast Repertory, Costa Mesa). The play received numerous awards, including the American Theatre Critics Association New Play Award, The Dramatists Guild/Hull-Warriner Award, the Lucille Lortel Award, the Outer Critics Circle Award and a Drama Desk nomination.

His many plays include *Shipwrecked! An Entertainment—The Amazing Adventures of Louis de Rougemont (As Told by Himself)* (Geffen Playhouse, Los Angeles; South Coast Repertory; Primary Stages, New York); *Brooklyn Boy* (Manhattan Theatre Club, New York; South Coast Repertory; Comedie des Champs-Elysées), which was an American Theatre Critics Association New Play Award finalist and an Outer Critics Circle nominee; *Sight Unseen* (Manhattan Theatre Club; South Coast Repertory; Comedie des Champs-Elysées), which received an OBIE Award, The Dramatists Guild/Hull-Warriner Award, a Drama Desk nomination, and was a Pulitzer Prize finalist; *Collected Stories* (Theatre Royal Haymarket, London; South Coast Repertory; Manhattan Theatre Club; HB Studio/Lucille Lortel Theatre, New York), which received the Los Angeles Drama Critics Circle/Ted Schmitt Award, the L.A. Ovation Award, a Drama Desk nomination, and which was a finalist for The Dramatists Guild/Hull-Warriner Award and the Pulitzer Prize; *God of Vengeance* (based on the Yiddish classic by Sholom Asch; produced by ACT Theatre, Seattle; Williamstown

Theatre Festival, Massachusetts); *Two Days* (Long Wharf Theatre, New Haven); *The Model Apartment* (Los Angeles Theatre Center; Primary Stages; La Jolla Playhouse; Long Wharf Theatre), which won an OBIE Award, a Drama-Logue Award, and was a Dramatists Guild/Hull-Warriner Award finalist and a Drama Desk nominee; *The Loman Family Picnic* (Manhattan Theatre Club), which was a Drama Desk nominee; *What's Wrong with This Picture?* (Manhattan Theatre Club; Jewish Repertory Theatre, New York; Brooks Atkinson Theatre, New York); *Broken Sleep: Three Plays* (Williamstown Theatre Festival); *July 7, 1994* (Actors Theatre of Louisville); *Found a Peanut* (The Joseph Papp Public Theater/New York Shakespeare Festival); *Pitching to the Star* (West Bank Café, New York); *Resting Place* (Theatre for the New City, New York); *Gifted Children*; *Zimmer* and *Luna Park* (Jewish Repertory Theatre).

Dinner with Friends was made into an Emmy Award–nominated film for HBO, and *Collected Stories* was presented on PBS.

Mr. Margulies has received grants from the National Endowment for the Arts, the New York Foundation for the Arts, and the John Simon Guggenheim Memorial Foundation. He was the recipient of the 2000 Sidney Kingsley Award for Outstanding Achievement in the Theatre. In 2005 he was honored by the American Academy of Arts and Letters with an Award in Literature and by the National Foundation for Jewish Culture with its Award in Literary Arts. Mr. Margulies is an alumnus of New Dramatists and serves on the council of The Dramatists Guild of America.

Born in Brooklyn, New York, in 1954, Mr. Margulies now lives with his wife, Lynn Street, a physician, and their son, Miles, in New Haven, Connecticut, where he is an adjunct professor of English and Theatre Studies at Yale University.

ABOUT THE COVER PHOTOGRAPH

Fallujah, Iraq. Iraqi men bury the bodies of five men allegedly killed in an explosion in a mosque in Fallujah, some thirty km west of Baghdad, July 1, 2003. Iraqis in Fallujah claim that American forces dropped a missile on the mosque the night before. The case is currently under investigation.

Lynsey Addario, photographer / lynseyaddario.com

CPSIA information can be obtained
at www.ICGtesting.com
Printed in the USA
JSHW020948060223
37299JS00003B/4